Words That Change Minds

Mastering the Language of Influence

Second Edition

Shelle

Withdrawn

KENDALL/HUNT PUBLISHING COMPANY
4050 Westmark Drive   Dubuque, Iowa 52002

To my sons, Jason and Sammy,
who give me much joy and keep on teaching me,
to my Mum, Betty Rose,
for always being there,
in memory of my Dad, Frank Rose,
who taught me about intellectual rigour and humour,
and in memory of my Grandma, Katie Rose,
who kept asking me: "Who told you?"

Copyright © 1995, 1997 by Shelle Rose Charvet, Success Strategies

Library of Congress Catalog Card Number: 97-70788

ISBN: 0-7872-3479-6

Printed in the United States of America
10   9   8   7   6   5   4

"I pull out *Words That Change Minds* whenever I am facing a situation where I am not connecting with an individual. By using Shelle's techniques I can understand them better and then establish a much higher level of rapport. As a sales professional there are times when I have to present to key decision makers. Shelle's book has helped me understand how to communicate with people on their terms and that has increased sales."

—Karl Meema,
Prairie Regional Manager, Microsoft Canada Inc.,
Calgary, Alberta

"*Words That Change Minds* belongs on the must read list for everyone who interacts with other people. I have found it to be invaluable for understanding and communicating effectively with business associates, family and friends. It's the first book I have read that identifies various styles of communicating and outlines an easy-to-follow process to create an accurate exchange of information."

—Tom Dearth,
President, Spotlight Presentations,
Denver, Colorado

"Shelle's book, *Words That Change Minds*, is a helpful and practical reference tool and guide in preparation for management, negotiation, mediation or conflict resolution. Understanding and respecting people is at the core of good communications. I have found the LAB Profile to be a useful and insightful tool. It helps you progress towards your desired outcome, while respecting the needs and pace of those with whom you are working."

—Geneviève O'Sullivan,
Director General, Strategic & Corporate Relations,
Agriculture and Agri-food Canada, Ottawa, Ontario

"I read the book during a ski trip in New Zealand—it's easy reading, entertaining, and very practical. I've used the motivation traits questions to help a Malaysian friend clarify his career goals, a middle-age friend to build her résumé, and most interesting of all, a Chinese lady to decide whether or not she should buy a South Sea pearl necklace! And all the while, they didn't know I was using the standard questions because it was like natural conversation."

—Kenzie L. Kwong,
Director, Kenn & K Consulting Ltd.,
Hong Kong and Asia Pacific

"This book provides intriguing insights into what motivates people, how they make decisions and generally what makes them tick. I found this information very valuable."

—Juel Hogg
Marketing Program Manager,
Hewlett-Packard, (Canada) Ltd.,
Toronto, Ontario

"*Words That Change Minds* has greatly assisted our staff in honing their negotiating skills—I highly recommend this book to anyone who has to deal with high stakes communication."

—Harry Hynd
Director, District 6, United Steelworkers of America,
Toronto, Ontario

"Knowing the precise definitions of spoken or written words is not enough to understand the real intended meaning. The LAB Profile solves this for each unique relationship and provides the influencing words that are most effective for that particular relationship."

—Chuck Watson
Corporate Accounts Vice President, Coulter Corporation,
Miami, Florida

"Excellent book—would recommend this book to anyone wanting to use NLP in the business world. Written in a down-to-earth, extremely readable, interesting style with useful real-world examples . . . and with a great sense of humor!"

—David Kintler,
President, SalesWinners, Inc.
Coral Springs, Florida

"After reading Shelle's book, I asked her to train my management, customer service representatives, consultants and sales staff. Not only does it work in achieving bottom line results in business, she also taught my wife and I how to communicate at a new level. Shelle is the master of influential communication. I strongly urge all business leaders to read this book . . . it could change your life!"

—Richard A. Grehalva,
Vice President, CSC Health Care Systems,
Birmingham, Alabama

Contents

Part 1   **Introduction**   **1**

Introduction   3
    History of the LAB Profile   7
    Meta Programs   11

Part 2   **Motivation Traits**   **15**

Motivation Traits   17

Waiting for Godot or Jumping at the Bit:
    Motivation Level   19
      Proactive   19
      Reactive   19
      Stepping on Toes: People Management   22
      Fate and Destiny   22
      Sales and Marketing   23
      Golden Handshakes   23

Pushing Those Hot Buttons: Criteria   25
    What to Do with Criteria   26
    Influencing with Criteria:
      A Powerful Sales and Marketing Tool   31

The Carrot or the Stick:
    Motivation Direction   33
      Toward   33
      Away From   33
      So, Why *Did* You Leave Your Last Job?   36
      Is It Fear of Success or
       Motivation Direction?   38
      Positive or Negative Thinking?   39
      Conflicts of Language in
       Labour Relations   39
      Professions Have Cultures   40
      The Cure to Writers' Block   43

The Margaret Thatchers of the World:
Motivation Source   49
   Internal   49
   External   50
   Where Do You Know That?   52
   Margaret Thatcher   53
   Brian Mulroney, Michael Wilson, the GST,
     and Free Trade   53
   Making Criticism and Responding to
     Feedback   54
   What Self-Esteem Is Not   55
   Selling in a Buyer's Market: Adapting to the
     Shift in Customers   58
   Doctors and Patients   60

Sometimes You Just Gotta Break the Rules:
Motivation Reason   63
   Options   63
   Procedures   63
   Culture Clashes at Work   69
   Total Quality Management?   73
   Learning New Skills, or Why Some of Us
     Can't Understand Computer Nerds   69
   Working with Groups   74

When the Bell Tolls: Motivation Decision
Factors   77
   Sameness   77
   Sameness with Exception   77
   Difference   77
   Sameness with Exception and
     Difference   78
   Making Your Change Pattern Work
     for You   80
   Revolutions and Evolutions: Hiring   82
   Taking the Pain out of Organizational
     Change   83
   Why New Coke Didn't Make It   84
   Purchasers and Users of Software   85

Using the Profiling Worksheet:
Motivation Traits   87
   Giving Feedback   87

The LAB Worksheet: Motivation Traits   89

Part **3 Working Traits 91**

Working Traits   93

The Forest for the Trees: Working Scope   95
    Specific   95
    General   96
    When Bad Communication Happens to
        Good People   98
    Why Do All the Songs I Know End in
        La, La, La?   99
    Difficult Bosses   100
    Life, the Universe, and Everything   101
    Pies in the Sky   101

When Hinting Won't Work: Working Attention
    Direction   103
    Self   103
    Other   103
    One in Fourteen People   104
    Once a Self, Always a Self?   106

Freaked Out or Cool as a Cucumber: Working
    Stress Response   109
    Feeling   109
    Choice   109
    Thinking   110
    Incompetency Attacks   112
    Passion   112
    Managing Stress and People   112
    Language Range and Culture   114

I Wanna Do It *Myself*: Working Style   117
    Independent   117
    Proximity   117
    Co-operative   118
    Team Players? Hiring and
        People Management   120

Facts and Feelings: Working Organization   123
    Person   123
    Thing   123
    Good and Bad People?   125
    Intimate Relationships   127

Why Middle Management Got the Squeeze
When the Crunch Came: Working Rule
Structure   129
  My/My   129
  My/.   129
  No/My   130
  My/Your   130
  So, Why Did Middle Management Get the
    Squeeze?   132
  Telling Yourself What to Do   133
  Raising Kids   133

Decision Making Processes:
  Convincer Channel   135
    Channel Patterns   135

Clinching the Deal: Convincer Mode   139
    Tough Customers   143

The LAB Profile Worksheet: Working Traits   147

Part 4 Applications   149

Applications   151

Career Counselling and Personal Profiles   153

Corporate Culture Diagnosis and
  Change Measurement   161

Hiring Employees Who Perform   163
  Job Profiles   163
  Attracting Only the Right People: Career
    Advertisements   169

Building a High-Performance Team   171

Negotiating and Bargaining   175
  Preparation Is the Key   176

Hitting the Target: Analyzing Your Market   177
  Market Research   178

Sales, Sales and More Sales   181
  Who Can Sell and Who Can't?   182

Political Campaigns   183
  The Notwithstanding Clause   183

Education and Learning   185
   Adult Learners   186
Default Profiles   189
What Else?   191

Appendices   193

Summaries and Useful Bits   195
Lab Profile Pattern Summary   197
Pattern Distribution   201
Influencing Language Summary   203
Research Abstracts   207
Resources   211
LAB Profile Worksheets   213
Index   217

Acknowledgments

I would like to thank all those people, too numerous to name, who helped make this book possible by developing the original ideas, giving me valuable learning experiences, sharing with me their expert opinions and feedback, and allowing me to work and play with them, in personal and professional relationships.

Thank you to Richard Bandler, John Grinder, Leslie Cameron-Bandler, and Judith Delozier for their development of Neuro-linguistic Programming. A BIG thank you to Rodger Bailey for his creation of the Language and Behaviour Profile, which is the basis of this book and much of my work. And thanks to all the other developers, teachers, and practitioners of NLP who have influenced my life and my work.

I would like particularly to thank Dr. Lorraine Bourque, from the Faculty of Education at the Université de Moncton in Moncton, New Brunswick, for her insight, feedback, and friendship. Micheline Sirois and Étienne Godin from the same university contributed their research abstracts to the second edition. Many thanks to Dr. David Rosenbloom, head of pharmaceutical services at Chedoke-McMaster Hospitals in Hamilton, Ontario, for his ability to see and realize the potential of new ideas; and Doug MacPherson, assistant to the director of District 6 of the United Steelworkers of America, for his feedback and support of my work. Thanks to Thelma Egerton of IBM Europe for being a great client and friend, as well as a great trainer, who has shared many laughs and a few tears with me over the years. And a big "Merci!" to Pierre Artigues (Señor), my former boss in Paris and always my friend, for teaching me more about intellectual rigour and helping me understand and adapt to living and working in France. Thanks to Steven Robbins and Joseph O'Connor for their help editing my clumsy prose in the second edition. Thanks also to the many readers who enthusiastically contacted me with ideas and suggestions, many of which have been included in the second edition.

Thanks to Ainslie Smith for reading what I wrote on her island paradise in Georgian Bay and saying it was great. Thanks to Stever and Jay Arthur for their excellent ideas for a book title, and to Michael Erdos for cover ideas.

Most of all I wish to thank my family: my brothers, Michael Rose (my computer guru) and Professor Jonathan Rose, for learning and using the material and encouraging me to write the book; my sister-in-law, award-winning writer Barbara Wade Rose, for her personal support and critical eye; my mother, Betty Rose, for helping out in many ways; my kids, Jason and Sammy, for being who they are. All my family for loving and encouraging me. I love you all.

Part 1

Introduction

𝒞ntroduction

≈≈≈

Cheryl walked into my office for her appointment looking frustrated and angry. A well-dressed, elegant professional, she did not waste a second on the customary niceties of a first encounter.

"I need to find a new job right away," she said. "I can't stand my boss and I heard that you do career profiles." After some discussion about what she wanted and what was important to her, we agreed to do a career profile. About halfway though the feedback on the profile she called a halt to the whole process. "Oh my God," she said. "My boss and I are obstinate in exactly the same way! We are constantly arguing. Neither of us will budge from our positions. No wonder we haven't been getting along! Can you show me how to communicate with him?" I took a few minutes and taught her the exact language to use and avoid. Within two months she called to tell me of a major promotion she had just received. Today she is one of the highest-ranking women in her sector in the country.

Poor communication is today's number one problem at work, at home, and in the world at large. Discords among people are frequent, from small annoyances like twenty-minute phone mail messages, to lifelong parent-child resentments, to intractable conflicts between nations. Finding solutions to communication problems has been the focus of much study and the development of many models.

Many psychometric assessments have been created to explain the differences that cause communication problems between people. These assessments often require sophisticated computerized instruments to administer. Even then, many of them only allow a few very specialized applications, or worse, stick people in boxes with labels, like round pegs into square holes. Often they do not recognize people's inherent flexibility to shift thinking and behaviour as situations change. It is not surprising that a great many individuals, while fascinated by questionnaires, tend to discount the sweeping generalizations these instruments produce. People often prefer to rely solely on their intuition and gut feelings to make critical decisions such as hiring or choosing a spouse. I once told a CEO that if he hired his executive vice president because he *liked* the person, he would be in big trouble. The last thing he needed was to recruit someone who thought just like he did.

3

It is well known that people communicate through a set of filters shaped by history, sense of identity, beliefs about what is true, and values about what is right, as well as perceptions and interpretations of what is going on. When someone else communicates with us, we squeeze the message through our own personal filtering system to understand. Of course, people from the same ethnic, cultural, gender, national, or geographic grouping have some common history and beliefs. That makes communication within a group easier than between people who come from different backgrounds.

We are now beginning to grasp that, beyond these differences, each of us also has unique *ways* of thinking and processing. We pay attention to various aspects of reality, based on how we *individually* use our brains. Some of us think in detailed linear sequences, while others prefer to envision a larger whole. Some people are attracted to those things that are different and new, while others attend to what is the same or similar to what they already know.

But what if we *could* really understand what someone means when he or she talks to us? Even better, what if we could predict someone's behaviour based simply on what was said? Best of all—what if we could *influence* that behaviour by how we responded?

I investigated the field to find some answers to these complex questions of understanding, communicating, and influencing. I wanted to avoid facile solutions. Any good theory must be well founded and verifiable by personal experience. It must also be applicable for a wide range of human activities, respectful of individual people and their differences, and learnable without a doctorate or engineering degree. Above all, it had to improve communication between people.

In 1983, while teaching communication seminars in Europe, I started to hear about some interesting work that came from (wouldn't you know it) California. I began to explore this approach, called Neuro-linguistic Programming (NLP). In spite of its techno-babble name, it seemed to be designed to reach into people's minds and discover how specifically each person is unique. It was based on studying some of the great communicators and therapists of our time. It examined *how* they were able to accomplish what they did, without the usual investigation into the reasons *why* people have problems. It was about learning strategies that work, not about scrutinizing the failures that people experience.

I wanted to find out if these people were onto something. I took some in-depth courses and began to test their techniques in my work. The results were remarkable. I learned how to create rapport with anyone, to change beliefs that had been limiting me, and to help others do the same. Being a doubting Thomas, I liked the requirement that every intervention be tested for possible negative consequences prior to being completed with a person. If someone were actually to let go of the belief that rainy days make them sick, a practitioner would have to check first if getting sick on rainy days had some positive benefits that needed to be met in some other healthier way for the person, *before* helping him replace the belief.

In 1985 I encountered a specific tool developed from NLP that completely changed the way I communicate. It is both rigourous and flexible. It can be woven naturally into casual conversation. I have spent the years since then exploring its uses in a wide range of contexts. I have used it to:

- create powerful presentations for large groups of people
- redesign marketing and sales processes to help companies successfully reach their major customers
- attract and select only the right candidates for key executive positions
- help clients I coached or counselled
- create *irresistible* influencing language for teenagers, and
- help organizations dramatically improve their communication about change with their own people.

While this tool has been widely taught, it had been treated as an abstract theory about the differences between people. I kept finding new ways of applying it and getting dramatic results. I wondered why no one had written a book on all the things you could do with it, provided you took the time to master the skill. This book is the result of testing it out for myself and with my clients.

In 1995 and 1996 I assisted in the supervision of two Master of Education theses. One thesis succeeded in establishing the reliability of the tool, and the other investigated whether there were predictable patterns in people who were able to make career decisions, compared with people who found it difficult or impossible to decide on a career. I have included the research abstracts in the appendices.

The Language and Behaviour Profile (LAB Profile)

The tool is called the **Language and Behaviour Profile (LAB Profile)**. It is a way of thinking about people and groups that allows you to notice and respond to how they get motivated, process information, and make decisions.

It is a set of about a dozen questions that you can feed into casual conversation or use as a formal survey for groups. You pay attention to *how* people talk when they answer, rather than *what* they talk about. Even when a person does not answer the question directly, he will reveal his pattern by the manner in which he answers (or doesn't).

As you become familiar with the questions and the kind of responses people give, you will find that you can hear and pick up the patterns people use without having to actually ask the questions. You can immediately use the Influencing Language that is just right for the situation. People communicate with their particular patterns naturally as they speak, both in words and in their body language, and they respond immediately when you use *their* language.

Because the LAB Profile can be used informally in conversation, I have included in this book many sample conversations. To illustrate the kind of emphasis and inflection that we typically employ when we talk, I have made liberal use of **bold** and *italic* characters.

As you read this book, check it out with your own experience, relating it to the people you know, recognizing yourself and others. I hope you will find some solutions to the challenges you face as you communicate with people on a daily basis. Even if you do not have specific communication problems, this book will provide you with useful information to consider and a vocabulary for describing what you are already doing—perhaps unconsciously.

I keep discovering new insights and uses for this material both in my personal life and in my work. I invite you to join with me in exploring the possible applications of the LAB Profile.

$\mathcal{H}$istory of the LAB Profile

Words That Change Minds is built on the Language and Behaviour Profile, or LAB Profile, created by Rodger Bailey. The LAB Profile is a development based on specific applications from *Neuro-linguistic Programming*, a field developed by Richard Bandler, John Grinder, and others in the United States, beginning in the mid-70s. They created the original models of Neuro-linguistic Programming (or NLP) by examining and understanding the processes used by highly successful communicators.

The field of NLP has been expanding exponentially since then, and is now the subject of hundreds of books written around the world. This approach is being taught in several dozen countries on all five continents. For those of you unfamiliar with Neuro-linguistic Programming, here is my own brief definition of what it is.[1]

Let's start with Programming. Each person, through genetic makeup, environmental influences, and individual biochemistry, has managed to *program* herself or himself to be excellent at a certain number of things, mediocre at different things, and just awful in other areas.

If we observe and listen carefully to how a person behaves and communicates *linguistically*, we can glean an understanding of how, *neurologically*, a person puts his or her experience together to be excellent, mediocre, or awful at the things he or she does. Hence, this field is called Neuro-linguistic Programming.

The applications are enormous. It means if someone is highly skilled at something, a person trained in certain NLP protocols can *model* her. Modelling is finding out how it is possible for that person to do what she does. The modeller searches for the answers to questions such as: "What are the absolute essentials?" or "What is that person paying attention to or ignoring, sequentially and/or simultaneously, to be able to do it?" When the answers to these and other questions are found, then it becomes possible to teach that skill to other people, and even learn it oneself.

The Language and Behaviour Profile is a model created by Rodger Bailey, an avid developer in the field of NLP. He created the LAB Profile in the

---

1. For a very complete introduction to NLP, see **Introducing NLP**, by Joseph O'Connor and John Seymour, (London: HarperCollins, 1993).

early 1980s. It is based on set of patterns from NLP called, at the time they were developed, the *Meta Programs*. These Meta Programs are based on the filters that we use to make up our *model of the world*.

Creating Our Model of the World

Every person has a certain number of filters by which they let in certain parts of the real world. In Noam Chomsky's 1957 Ph.D. thesis, *Transformational Grammar*, he said there are three processes by which people create the filters of their individual Model of the World:

Deletion

The first process is called **deletion**. We delete lots of information from the environment around us and internally. In his 1956 paper entitled **Seven Plus or Minus Two**, George Miller, an American psychologist, said that our conscious minds can only handle seven plus-or-minus two bits of information at any one time, and that we delete the rest. That means on a good day we can deal with nine bits and on a bad day, maybe only five.

This explains why most telephone numbers are a maximum of seven digits. However, while I was living in Paris in the 1980s, they changed the phone numbers to eight digits. Everyone then had to decide whether to remember phone numbers by groups of two, or four, or to simply add the new Paris code, 4, onto the front of their old number. No one had an easy way of keeping eight digits in their head at once. Each person had to find their own way to break it down. People would give out their new phone numbers in their own peculiar manner. It created a great deal of confusion.

So seven plus or minus two bits of information is what we can be comfortably be aware of at one time. Using the process of deletion, we filter out lots of things without being aware of it or consciously choosing to do so.

Distortion

The second process is called **distortion**. We distort things. Have you ever moved to a new place and gone into the living room before you moved your things in and pictured what it was going to look like furnished? Well, you were hallucinating. Your furniture was not *actually* in the room, was it? So you were distorting Reality.

Two examples of distortion are hallucination and creativity. They are both similar in that the external information is changed to something else. That is what the process of distortion is all about.

Generalization

Chomsky's third mental filtering process is called **generalization**. It is the opposite of Cartesian Logic (where you can go from a general rule to specific examples but not the other way around). Generalization is where you take a few examples and then create a general principle. This is how learning occurs. A small child learns to open one or two, or possibly three, doors and then she knows how to open all doors. The child develops a Generalization about how to open doors. That is, until she has to enter a high-tech company and realizes that, to open the door, there is a magnetic card that has to be slid down a slot in a certain way. She has to relearn how to open doors to deal with those exceptions.

Generalization is about how we unconsciously generate rules, beliefs, and principles about what is true, untrue, possible, and impossible. Some women, for example, may have had several bad experiences with men and then come to the conclusion that men (i.e., *all* men) cannot be trusted. They develop the rule: *Never trust a man*. People have a certain number of experiences of a similar type and then make a rule or develop a belief.

With the three filters, Deletion, Distortion and Generalization, we each create our own model of the world.

Meta Programs

≋

What is the link between these three processes—NLP, The Meta Programs, and the LAB Profile? The co-originators of NLP used Chomsky's Deletion, Distortion and Generalization model to create a map for discovering and influencing a person's perceptions and interpretations of their experiences.[2]

Leslie Cameron-Bandler took Chomsky's work even further. She postulated that each person makes specific kinds of Deletions, Distortions and Generalizations, which then show up in a person's behaviour. From her work in therapeutic settings, she identified about sixty different patterns, which she called Meta Programs.

Meta Programs are the specific filters we use to interact with the world. They edit and shape what we allow to come in from the outside world. They also mould what comes from inside ourselves as we communicate and behave in the world.

Meta Programs are like a door through which we interact with the world. This door has a particular shape and has the power to let only certain things in or out. This may appear to be part of our individual nature, and therefore permanent; in fact, the door itself can shift in response to changes in ourselves and our surrounding environment.

Rodger Bailey, a student of Leslie's, adapted and used her work in business settings. He created the LAB Profile, which enables us to understand what people are communicating about their reality when they talk. He said that the Meta Programs are a status report on how a person responds to a given situation. Most people would agree that our behaviour is different when we are with different people, at work, or at home with our family. The Meta Programs are not, therefore, descriptions of our *personality* as such, but rather a picture of how we interact with different environments or contexts.

The Meta Programs simply describe the form of our door, what specifically we let in and out in a given situation. It is this recognition of our ability to change our behaviour that sets this tool apart from the psychometric profiles that make sweeping generalizations about our personality.

---

2. Their map is called **The Meta Model.** Please see **The Structure of Magic 1** by Richard Bandler and John Grinder (Science and Behaviour Books, 1975).

Language and Behaviour Patterns

When I first learned about Meta Programs, there were about sixty patterns. We had to talk to the people we were studying with and *guess* what their patterns were. I spent a year and a half trying to guess what everyone's Meta Programs were, and needless to say, I was not very good at it.

To make detecting and using these patterns simpler, Rodger Bailey had the foresight to reduce the number of patterns from sixty to fourteen. (Do you really need to know sixty things about yourself or another person?) He also developed a small set of specific questions by which, regardless of what people answer, their unconscious patterns are revealed *in the structure* of the language they use. You pay attention to *how* people answer, instead of *what* they say. In this way, after asking a few simple questions, you can determine what will *trigger and maintain* someone's motivation and how they internally process information.

He identified two separate kinds of Meta Programs when he developed the LAB Profile. He called the first set of categories **Motivation Traits**. These are the patterns that indicate what a person needs to get and stay motivated in a given Context, or conversely what will demotivate someone. Sometimes I call these the Motivation Triggers because they reveal what will *make* a person do something or *prevent* a person from acting in a certain way.

Rodger Bailey called the second set **Working Traits**. These categories describe the internal mental processing that a person uses in a specific situation. For example, we can determine if a person prefers an overview or sequential details, the environments in which she is most productive, whether a person attends to people or tasks, how she responds to stress, and the mechanics that lead her to becoming convinced about something.

And all this shows up in *how* a person talks.

Influencing Language

He also developed the *Influencing Language*. Once you know a person's patterns, you can then tailor your language so that it has *maximum impact* for that person.

Imagine for a moment that someone who did not master your mother tongue very well was attempting to get some ideas across to you. Chances are that you would spend a lot of energy translating it into terms that were more meaningful to you. When someone uses terms that you can *immediately* understand, none of your energy is lost in translating; the meaning just goes in. When you use the appropriate Influencing Language, the impact is powerful precisely because you are *speaking in someone's own personal style*.

You can choose exactly those **words that change minds**.

Reality

I need to make another point before we go on, just to avoid any confusion. From Noam Chomsky and many others, we know that people do not actually live in Reality. By deleting, distorting and generalizing, we inhabit our *perceptions* and *interpretations* of Reality. The LAB Profile patterns reflect a person's Model of the World.

Because of this, I will NOT generally be dealing with Reality in this book, but rather the way we *perceive and interpret* it. As John Lennon said: "Reality leaves a lot to the imagination." On the other hand, Woody Allen said: "Reality is the pits, but it's the only place you can get a good steak." Since we do need to eat, I will make reference to Reality from time to time; the occasional Reality Check, so to speak.

How the LAB Profile Works in Communication

Let's say a person has an experience. When that person talks about his experience, he only communicates a minute portion of the actual event. He has to edit out the vast majority of what was going on for him, just to be able to communicate it in a reasonable time frame. It means that in order for you to tell someone about reading this book, you will need to eliminate most of what you experienced. You might say, "It was good," and nod your head, perhaps leaving out all the things this book made you think about, not mentioning whether you were physically comfortable at the time you were reading. Think of all those times when you did not grasp what someone was talking about because they left out elements you needed to fully understand.

People transform their actual experience, their opinions, and so on, in ways that correspond to their own particular Deletions, Distortions, and Generalizations.

Leslie Cameron-Bandler and Rodger Bailey determined that people who use the *same language patterns* in their speech have the *same behaviours*. The Language and Behaviour Profile got its name from the connections between a person's language and how they behave.

The tools in this book will enable you to *understand, predict* and *influence* behaviour. The LAB Profile is a set of tools that can be learned as a skill. You will have the opportunity to train your eyes and ears to perceive certain things that you may not have paid attention to before. You will also learn some ways of describing and working with behaviour patterns you may have already noticed.

Because the LAB Profile is a set of skills, you will need to use it with rigour, paying attention to the shifts people make as they move from situation to situation. This is where the notion of Context comes in.

Context

The Context is the frame of reference a person puts around a situation. Since human beings are flexible by nature, they are able to behave differently at different times. Are we talking about you at work, in a couple relationship, with your kids, with your peers, when you are on holiday, or when you are buying a house? Simply because a person has a certain pattern (or habit) in a given place and time does not indicate that she will have that same pattern in another Context.

When I run seminars in this material, people ask me: "Am I always that way?" The answer is no. We move, we grow, and our response to significant events in our lives can change how we function. These changes show up in the LAB Profile patterns we use in conversation. Because our behaviour can vary in different situations, you will need to make sure when using the LAB Profile questions, that you have clearly and specifically identified the Context. What is the frame of reference (or Context) around the situation for the person you are speaking with? I will demonstrate how specifically to do this as we discuss each pattern.

If used with integrity and care, the LAB Profile will enable you to improve your communication dramatically in many Contexts. It will enable you to adapt what you do to fit any situation.

The tools in this book will not only aid you in thinking about how you communicate, but will actually help you become a better communicator. They will enable you to prevent and avoid problems that you might not otherwise have foreseen. You will save time as you move more quickly toward your goals. You will become aware of the results, and others are sure to notice the difference. These tools will help you progress in your growth, or totally change the things you want.

Think of what you'll achieve as you master those *Words That Change Minds*.

Part **2**

Motivation Traits

Motivation Traits

≈

Questions	Categories	Patterns—Indicators
(no question for Level)	**LEVEL** _____ _____	**Proactive**—*action, do it, short, crisp sentences* **Reactive**—*try, think about it, could, wait*
• **What do you want in your (*work*)?**	**CRITERIA**	
• **Why is that (*criteria*) important?** (ask up to 3 times)	**DIRECTION** _____ _____	**Toward**—*attain, gain, achieve, get, include* **Away From**—*avoid, exclude, recognize problems*
• **How do you know you have done a good job (*at . . .*)?**	**SOURCE** _____ _____	**Internal**—*knows within self* **External**—*told by others, facts and figures*
• **Why did you choose (*your current work*)?**	**REASON** _____ _____	**Options**—*criteria, choice, possibilities, variety* **Procedures**—*story, how, necessity, didn't choose*
• **What is the relationship between (*your work this year and last year*)?**	**DECISION FACTORS** _____ _____ _____ _____	**Sameness**—*same, no change* **Sameness with Exception**—*more, better, comparisons* **Difference**—*change, new, unique* **Sameness with Exception & Difference**—*new and comparisons*

Motivation Traits

≈≈≈

The first six categories in the LAB Profile will show you how different people trigger their motivation and what language you will need to use to capture their interest. Each category is dealt with in a separate chapter.

For each category of patterns you will learn the questions to ask, how to detect the patterns in ordinary conversation, what each person needs to get interested or excited about something, and conversely, what would turn them off.

There are no good or bad patterns to have. You can judge the appropriateness of each pattern only in the Context of the activity that needs to be done. For each pattern I have included ways to take advantage of the strengths and qualities inherent in each one.

While each category represents behaviour on a *continuum* from one pattern to another, **each pattern is described in its pure form. Behaviour predictions are only valid in the same Context in which the subject was profiled**.

After the behaviour description for each pattern you will find a section entitled **Influencing Language**. Listed here are examples of the kind of language that has the greatest impact. For each category, the distribution of the patterns is shown. The figures are from the research that Rodger Bailey conducted, and refer only to the Context of work. They will give you an idea of how frequently you can expect to find certain patterns.

I will discuss the patterns in different situations, with lots of examples to provide insight and illustrate the fine points of using *Words That Change Minds*.

At the end of both the Motivation Traits and Working Traits sections are **summary worksheets**, which can be used when profiling people. At the end of the book are complete profiling worksheets.

Waiting for Godot or Jumping at the Bit: Motivation Level

> *Does the person take the initiative or wait for others?*

This category in the Motivation Traits is about what will get you going and what will make you think. What is your LEVEL of activity? There are two patterns:

Proactive

Proactive people initiate. They tend to act with little or no consideration, to jump into situations without thinking or analyzing. They may upset some people because they can bulldoze ahead with what they want to do. They are good at going out and getting the job done. They do not wait for others to initiate.

Reactive

Reactive people wait for others to initiate or wait until the situation is right before they act. They may consider and analyze without acting. They want to fully understand and assess the situation before they will act. They believe in chance and luck. They will spend a lot of time waiting. Some people may get upset with them because they do not *get started*. They will wait for others to initiate and then respond. In the extreme, they operate with extra caution and study situations endlessly. They make good analysts.

Distribution _____ %

(in the work Context, from Rodger Bailey)

Proactive	Equally Proactive & Reactive	Reactive
15–20%	60–65%	15–20%

Since about 60 to 65 percent of the population in the work Context have an equally Proactive and Reactive pattern, it is reasonable to assume that the person you are profiling is in the middle, unless they clearly demonstrate that they lean to one side or the other.

Pattern Recognition
≋

Since there is no specific question to ask for this category, you can pay attention to the person's sentence structure and body language, as they will be giving you their pattern throughout your conversation.

Proactive—sentence structure
- short sentences: noun, active verb, tangible object
- speaks as if they are in control of their world
- crisp and clear sentence structure
- direct
- at the extreme, they "bulldoze"

Proactive—body language
- signs of impatience, speaking quickly, pencil tapping, lots of movement or inability to sit for long periods

Reactive—sentence structure
- incomplete sentences, subject or verb missing
- passive verbs or verbs transformed into nouns
- lots of infinitives
- speak as if the world controls them, things happen to them, believe in chance or luck
- long and convoluted sentences
- talks about thinking about, analyzing, understanding, or waiting, or the principle of the thing
- conditionals, would, could, might, may
- overly cautious, need to understand and analyze

Reactive—body language
- willingness to sit for long periods

Examples

Proactive:	"I meet with my team every week."
Mainly Proactive:	"I meet with my team if it seems like we need it."
Equally Proactive and Reactive:	"I meet with my team to go over the current files. It is important to stay informed."
Mainly Reactive:	"Even though you might wonder if it is necessary

	to meet with the team every week, I do it because it is important that they feel they are being listened to."
Reactive:	"Even though everybody might wonder if it is really necessary to meet each week, it is important to consider the needs people have of being listened to."

Influencing Language

Just use these words and phrases to get people to jump into action. If you think about it, matching someone's way of being is very important when communicating.

Proactive
- go for it; just do it; jump in; why wait; now; right away; get it done; you'll get to do; take the initiative; take charge; run away with it; right now; what are you waiting for; let's hurry

Reactive
- let's think about it; now that you have analyzed it; you'll get to really understand; this will tell you why; consider this; this will clarify it for you; think about your response; you might consider; could; the time is ripe; good luck is coming your way

Since most people have some Proactive and Reactive, you can use both sets of Influencing Language; considering and doing.

Hiring

People who have a Proactive pattern at work are suitable for those positions that require taking the initiative, going out and getting it done. They would work well in outside sales, in independent businesses, or the kind of work where having *chutzpah*[1] is an asset. If you are advertising for a highly Proactive person, ask the applicants to phone instead of sending in a résumé. (Reactive people will not phone.)

People who have a Reactive pattern in the work Context are well suited to jobs that allow them to respond to requests. Representatives on customer service desks tend to be more Reactive. Many research and analytical jobs need someone who can spend a lot of time analyzing data.

Most people and most positions require a mixture of the two patterns. When hiring, you will need to examine what proportion of the work to be done consists of Reactive or Proactive activities, to determine the kind of balance you need. It is appropriate to profile the others on the team to make sure you have a good balance.

---

1. A Yiddish word, meaning having a lot of nerve

There are some *key questions* to ask yourself regarding this category when profiling a position. To what degree will this person need to take the initiative? How much of the job consists of responding, analyzing, or depending on the actions of others? You might want to estimate the percentage of overall time in Proactive or Reactive activities.

Stepping on Toes: People Management

People who have a strong Proactive pattern at work will be impatient with bureaucratic delays or internal politics, and may even go outside of their bounds, stepping on others' toes to get things done. They jump into activities and may go very far very fast, before you or they, notice when they are on the wrong track. As the manager of Proactive employees, you will need to channel their energy in appropriate directions. If they do not have the opportunity to use their high level of energy, they will become frustrated or bored, and as a result may use their initiative in unproductive ways. You can motivate them by giving them a job to do and telling them to "Go for it." You may need to remind them to think before they jump.

Reactive people will generally not take the initiative and will feel stressed or anxious when asked to do so. At the extreme, they will want to consider, analyze, and *be given* an understanding of situations almost to the exclusion of deciding or doing anything. In a team setting, Reactive people can contribute to the process by analyzing proposed solutions and slowing the process enough to consider ramifications and alternatives. You can motivate Reactive people by matching their pattern. "Now that you have had enough time to consider and think about this, I will need it on my desk by Monday at noon."

I recently discovered (by first-hand experience) how to drive Proactive people crazy. Put them in a situation that they dislike intensely, then make sure that they can do nothing about it.

Fate and Destiny

Reactive people do not believe that they control their world. Chances are that they will be waiting for someone else to solve problems or make improvements for them. Do you remember Vladimir and Estragon in Samuel Beckett's *Waiting for Godot*? They spent the entire play waiting for the mythical Godot to appear and solve all their problems.

Since most people at work are somewhere in the middle, they will need to think and do, respond and initiate. The best kinds of work for these people are tasks and responsibilities that allow enough of each. To motivate these people you would use both sets of Influencing Language. For example, "I would like you to think through what needs to be done and just go do it."

Sales and Marketing

Proactive people tend to buy when they get to do something right away. One day over coffee, I suggested doing a LAB Profile to help a prospective client decide on a career change. I told her that the profile would show her immediately what kinds of activities would trigger and maintain her motivation. She enthusiastically agreed and wanted to do it right then. As we were walking back to my office she said: "Can we run?" She has an off-the-scale Proactive pattern in that Context.

Reactive people will buy when the product or service allows them to gain understanding. They will often be waiting for something to happen before they will decide. I went to see the CEO of a company that sells mutual funds, to talk about sales training for his sales representatives. At our *third* meeting, he told me that the company was completing a merger and he was "waiting for the situation to be clarified." As a highly Proactive person, the voice in my head exploded and said, "What do you want, a message from God? *Who* is going to clarify the situation?" I managed to control the impulse and asked: "Oh, and when is this likely to happen?" I used that phrase to match his belief that things happen *to* him.

Reactive people will be more likely to buy if you suggest that this is what they have been waiting for, or "Haven't you waited long enough to get what you really want?" or "Once you have this, you'll understand why. . . . "

You will occasionally notice marketing campaigns that call to Proactive or Reactive people. These ads inadvertently may also be revealing aspects of the company's corporate culture. In 1993, a large Canadian bank had a slogan: "Get us working for you." My interpretation was that I, as a potential customer, was going to have to wake them up and make them do something for me. But perhaps that way of looking at it is a result of my propensity for being Proactive.

You may have noticed NIKE's slogan: "Just do it." It is a call to action for the Proactive sorts.

Golden Handshakes

During the early to mid-1990s, large corporations (and subsequently governments) decided they needed to shed large numbers of workers. In order to accomplish these large-scale layoffs, many organizations used the *Golden Handshake* approach, offering an attractive package to those who would take the money and leave.

Can you guess who took the money and jumped ship? Have you noticed that this period also coincided with the largest ever increase in home-based businesses?

Proactive people jump at the Golden Handshake as a chance to go out and set up their own operations. Organizations lost many of their most dynamic people. One friend told me that her boss said: "Oh, but we didn't want *you* to leave!" Too late, buddy.

My suggestion to organizations is to plan any necessary layoffs by first deciding *which roles to keep*. (Easier said than done, I know.) The roles will probably call for a mixture of Proactive and Reactive, as well as many of the other patterns described in this book. I then suggest that particular people be offered the buyout package: those who do not fit the desired profiles. Also, I believe it is important to offer counselling to those who will be leaving, to help them make decisions and set up their next steps.

——— Summary ———
≋

Level

Question: There is no question for this category.

Proactive: Acts with little or no consideration. Motivated by doing.
Reactive: Motivated to wait, analyze, consider and react.
Distribution
  at Work: Proactive 15–20%
             Equally 60–65%
             Reactive 15–20%

Influencing Language
Proactive: do it; jump in; get it done; don't wait; just do it; now
Reactive: understand; think about; wait; analyze; consider; wait; might; could; would

ᘲushing Those Hot Buttons: Criteria

≈≈≈

> *What are the words that will incite a physical and emotional response?*

I asked Simone: "What do you want in your work?" She replied: "*A challenge*, something that allows me to *utilize my present skills* and *develop new ones*, *good remuneration* and *working with people*."

Those are the things that are important to Simone in her work. Now what does this mean? Simone has given me her Criteria for work.

Criteria is the term we use to describe a person's way of making distinctions about what is good, bad, awful, wrong, right, and so on. They are personal labels. These words are the labels we give to our values.

A person's Criteria are those words that *incite a physical and emotional reaction*: **HOT BUTTONS**. The words themselves are associated, or stuck in our memory, to a series of emotionally similar events that we have experienced through our lives. So when a person hears one of her Criteria, *the word itself* will trigger the emotional response attached to it.

We each have our own definition for each Criterion. A single Criterion is composed of many elements, conscious and unconscious. You may never need to know a person's definition of her Criteria in those situations where you simply want to find out *how* she describes something she is excited about in a given Context.

In any family, each of you knows the others' negative hot buttons. The other members of your family know that if they say a particular word or phrase, you will explode. In my family, one son need only say to the other: "Nope, you're wrong!" to create an explosion of frustration, an emotional and physical reaction.

Many people took interpersonal communication courses in the 1970s and 80s and sometimes still today, where they learned Active Listening techniques, based on Carl Rogers' work. Active Listening consists of paraphrasing what the other person said, *in your own words*, in order to show him what you understood. We can now appreciate that if Simone says that she wants "a challenge" and I play back to her, "so you want something challenging," it does not *create* the same experience for her. When I paraphrase into my own words what you say, it has more to do with my reality than your reality, (and nothing whatever to do with Reality with a capital R). To solve this problem, we now teach participants in communication courses, that to show someone you have understood them, you will need to play back *their* key words, their Criteria.

Other questions to elicit Criteria:
- What do you want in . . . (a job, a home, a spouse, etc.)?
- What's important to you?
- What counts?
- What *has* to be there?
- What would you like to have, be or do?

What to Do with Criteria

Making Decisions: A Hierarchy of Criteria

Knowing how to uncover and work with Criteria can give you an infallible means of deciding what is more important and what is less important in a given Context. You can do this for yourself or with other people. I'll demonstrate with Simone. This technique is called making a **Hierarchy of Criteria.**

SRC:	Simone, you had a number of things that were important for you at work. Let's list them.
Simone:	A challenge, something that allows me to utilize my present skills and develop new ones, good remuneration, and working with people.

We have four Criteria here and we do not yet know which are essential, optional, or the most important for Simone. I, as the listener, may think one is more important than another for her, but that would be hallucinating.

SRC:	Simone, imagine for a moment that I have a couple of jobs that might fit your needs. In this hand over here (holding out my left hand, palm up), you will get a job with a *challenge*. And in this hand, (holding out my right hand, palm up, hands wide apart), this job allows you to *utilize your present skills and develop new ones*. Which one attracts you?
Simone:	A challenge.

If you observe carefully (which is *a challenge* to illustrate in a book) you can often see the choice being made before the person says anything. It is important to keep your hands wide apart so the person will perceive two *separate* choices. I do not know exactly how Simone is processing this choice, but by putting each option in a different hand, I am creating something more real or tangible for her.

How would I write down her choice if I were taking notes? An easy and quick way is to draw an arrow from *challenge* down to *allows me . . .* to indicate that "challenge" was chosen over "allows me."

SRC:	In my right hand is a job that will offer you *a challenge*. In my left is one that has *good remuneration*. If you **had** to choose, which one would you want?
Simone:	Hmmm. A challenge.
SRC:	So challenge is the most important so far. OK, in my left hand is a job with a *challenge* and in my right hand is a job where you'll be *working with people*. Which one would you prefer? (I keep switching the hand I put *challenge* in so as not create an association with one hand.)
Simone:	Still a challenge.

We now know that *a challenge* is the most important of these Criteria for Simone, in the Context of work. To complete the Hierarchy we will need to compare each of the other options to each other as we just did.

SRC:	Simone, in my left hand is a job that allows you to *utilize your present skills and develop new ones*, and in my right hand is one with *good remuneration*. Which one would you like to take?
S:	Good remuneration.
SRC:	And in my left hand we have one with *good remuneration* and, in my right hand, one where you can be *working with people*?
S:	Good remuneration.
SRC:	And lastly, *working with people* in my left hand, and *allows you to utilize your present skills and develop new ones* in my right hand?
S:	Working with people.

Now we have Simone's Criteria in order of importance to her:

1. A challenge
2. Good remuneration
3. Working with people
4. Allows me to utilize my present skills and develop new ones

For those of you who help people make decisions, as in sales, this is a very useful process to take your customers through. It can also be used when coaching employees or counselling clients. I also use it for career counselling, where I would also need to get the client to define what would constitute each Criterion.

The easiest way to get someone to define their Criteria is to ask: "Can you give me an example of something that was *a challenge*?" This works well because often people cannot give a straight definition of terms for something that is directly attached to a series of memories and emotions.

The Hierarchy of Criteria is also used to make some decision making processes much shorter. This is a way of helping people get their mind, soul, and body to decide. When you create a tangible, forced-choice situation, people will feel magnetically attracted to one option or the other.

Can't Make Up Your Mind?

Sometimes a person will have difficulty choosing between the two alternatives in your hands; you can confirm this by observing the vacillation in their body as they try to choose. What does this mean, and what do you do about it? There are five situations where this occurs that I have identified to date:

1. The person did not accept the idea that they *have* to choose between two things they want.
2. One Criterion is a component of the other one.
3. The person has two labels for the same set of experiences.
4. One Criterion causes the other to occur (a cause-effect relationship for the person).
5. The person has a conflict between two values or Criteria.

In the first case, if the person cannot or will not choose, you will need find a way to get them to play along. You can ask them to imagine that *if they **had** to choose*, knowing that in real life, they could actually have both, but if they *had* to choose, which one would attract them?

In teaching and working with the LAB Profile in different countries and cultures, I have noticed some cultural differences that may make it hard for some people to play along and choose which Criterion attracts them. In a culture where there is a belief that you *can* have anything you truly want (i.e., the United States), there is no problem in choosing.

Many cultures, however, do not maintain this belief. In fact, many people do not believe that life is *about* getting what you want. Life is about doing what you are *supposed* to do. The reason they cannot choose between Criteria is they believe that what they may want is irrelevant to what they are supposed to do. The weight of outside considerations is greater than their desires. When this is an issue in a group, we discuss what makes for

good decisions. If a person can be unburdened from his cares and obliga-
tions and, *just for a moment*, considers what appeals to him, he gets the
chance to sort out what is important to him. Then he can consider and
negotiate with his external commitments.

Sometimes they cannot choose because one Criterion is a component
of the other. In other words, one Criterion is *contained within* another Criterion. You can test for this by asking "Is *allows you to utilize your present skills
and develop new ones* part of a *challenge* for you? Or the other way around?"
In that case you can include the component within the larger Criterion and
only use the larger one. "So when we're talking about *a challenge,* we know it
includes *allows you to utilize your present skills and develop new ones.*"

Another possibility is that the person has two labels for the same set of
experiences. If it means the same thing, he would have difficulty choosing
between "it" and "itself." For example let's say a person cannot choose between *interesting* and *a challenge*. To test for this, you can simply ask: "Are
interesting and *a challenge* really the same thing for you?" If the persons says:
"Yes, it is always interesting when there's a challenge," you know that they
are closely linked (in his mind anyway). In this case you might want to use
both labels to stay in rapport with that person.

The fourth situation is when the person has the belief that one Criterion *causes* the other to occur in what is called a cause-effect relationship.
You can check for this by asking: "For you, does having *a challenge* make you
utilize your present skills and develop new ones?"

The fifth possibility for an unclear choice between two options presented in this manner is that the person has a conflict between two values
or Criteria. They will waver back and forth and "yes, but" to themselves or
out loud. You can predict, in this case, that the person will have difficulty
making certain decisions in this Context and will feel in a "stuck" state.
Remember Tevye in *Fiddler on the Roof*, "On one hand . . . on the other
hand . . . ?"

Difficult to Satisfy?

What does it mean when you ask someone "What do you want?" or
"What's important?" and the person lists fifteen or twenty things? It means
that this person is difficult to satisfy. If she has fifteen or twenty Criteria and
has no idea which ones are more important than the others, she will have a
difficult time making decisions or even being able to find exactly what she
wants. Can you imagine a woman finding the man of her dreams with fifteen Criteria?

What is a decision? Often making a decision consists of choosing between two or more alternatives. One of the biggest favours you can do for a
person who has many undifferentiated Criteria is to take him through a
Hierarchy of Criteria, and then have him create a bottom line cutoff point
on what absolutely must be there and what is optional.

Uses for Criteria

If you are considering buying a product, for example, what *must* it have? If you are considering getting married, what are the most important things for you in the person and the relationship? Remember that, when you change Context, your Criteria may change. Many people do not want the same thing in a house that they want in a spouse.

In the process of goal-setting, you need to list the Criteria for success, and understand which are more important. We know that those people who have clearly defined Criteria for their goals are more likely to achieve them quickly. By defining your Criteria, you will have made them real and tangible to yourself.

One of the gentlemen I trained in this technique is a Real Estate broker. When he hires people he uses the Hierarchy of Criteria to find out whether the candidates have the priorities about work that he would like them to have. He asks them "What is important for you in your work?" He then casually asks: "If you **had** to choose between a job where you got to be a *team player* (putting out his left hand) and one where you could be *your own boss* (putting out his other hand), which one would you pick?"

If you are going to start a project with someone or select members of a team or task force, you might want to check out what is important to each prospective member. Do they have the values you are looking for? You can ask them these questions: What do you want from this project? What do you want in a company? What do you want in a team? What's more important to you? This (holding out one hand) or this? You will find that it is very easy to build this into ordinary conversation.

I was a member of the advisory board of the local YMCA. Our highest ranking woman staff member quit the Association because she had been told that there was no possibility of a full-time executive director position at one of the local branches. As a result of her leaving, there was a reshuffle and suddenly a full-time executive director position was established. As a board member I hit the roof because of the unfairness of this.

The next thing I knew, I was in charge of a Committee that was to examine whether our Association had systemic barriers which prevented some employees from having the same opportunities as others. We were to make recommendations on how we could become a better employer.

We set some goals, defined the methodology, and then had to give the Committee a name. Some members suggested "The Employment Equity Committee," named after recently adopted legislation. I mentioned that many people (especially white males) had felt very threatened by this legislation and that, should we identify ourselves with it, we would get very little co-operation from the staff of the Y.

We named ourselves "The Fairness in Employment Committee" and got an 85 percent response rate when we distributed employee questionnaires. My point to the Committee was that we needed to call ourselves something with positive connotations for all staff, and make sure that we avoided any negative hot buttons.

Influencing with Criteria:
A Powerful Sales and Marketing Tool

The gathering of Criteria is a necessary prerequisite for sales and any kind of influencing or persuading process. Unskilled sales people just *pitch their product* (usually using their own Criteria) without much regard to what their prospective customer actually wants. "Lady, this car has everything you want: good mileage, great handling, and flashy decals on the side!" This is what I call the "shot in the dark" approach. Who knows? They might actually hit something.

Many market researchers investigate people's Criteria so that the exact phrasing of an advertising campaign can match what is most important to the groups they wish to influence.

If you want to get and keep someone's interest you will need to link what you are proposing with their Criteria. Often when I am giving a speech I do a question-and-answer session before I begin the body of my talk. I will often ask an audience "What's important to you when you communicate?" Or "If you knew how to understand, predict, and influence behaviour, what would you want to use this ability for?" If someone tells me they want to "know how to present their proposals in a negotiation so that they will be accepted," then I make sure to link those Criteria with the points I am making.

Many people underestimate the power of matching someone's Criteria. Once, as a demonstration with a group, I told a woman about a job opportunity, using all her highly held Criteria. I did not tell her what the job *was*; I simply used her Criteria: "You'll really be needed, people will appreciate what you do for them, you'll be in charge of how you work, and the hours are regular." She said she would take the job, without even finding out what it was.

I know someone who moved from New England to California for a career opportunity that *matched* his Criteria, only to find that the work and the company did not at all meet his expectations. You will need to be careful to deliver what you promise when you use someone's Criteria to persuade them. Otherwise their disappointment and anger likely will be directed at you. Just ask the leaders of all the governments thrown out of office by disenchanted voters.

In Grade One, my son was having difficulties learning to read. We practised at home and the teachers signed him up for the "Reading Club." Parent volunteers take members of the reading club out of class to help them with their reading skills. By the end of Grade One, my son had made *some* progress. He summed up his experience to me: "Only the stupid kids have to go to the reading club."

I met with the teachers at the beginning of Grade Two because they wanted Jason to join the club again. I explained to them what the *meaning* of the reading club was to my son and said that I didn't want him to join. After much discussion, they agreed, and I agreed to continue working with him. Two weeks later he said to me: "They didn't put me in the reading club this year. That's because I'm good at reading. And I'm not stupid." His reading skills picked up exceedingly quickly over the next few weeks.

Criteria are verbal triggers that bring up emotions, both positive and negative. Remember, in order to influence with Criteria, you will need to state them *exactly* as the other person expressed them.

Summary

≋≋

Criteria

A person's labels for things are important to them in a given Context. They are *hot buttons* because they are attached to emotions and memories.

Questions: What do you want in a . . . ? What is important to you?

Influencing Language

Use the person's Criteria to attract and maintain interest. When a person hears his own Criteria, he will immediately feel the emotions attached to those words.

The Carrot or the Stick: Motivation Direction

≈≈≈

> *What will trigger a person into action? In what direction do they move? Do they move* toward *an objective, or* away from *problems to be solved or prevented?*

When you master this category, you will be able to prevent and avoid many problems, and know how to reach your goals more effectively.

There are two patterns in this category describing the *Direction* a person is moving in for a given Context. They are either moving **toward** a goal, or **away from** problems. Each pattern is first described in its pure form.

Toward

People with a Toward pattern in a given Context are focused on their goal. They think in terms of goals to be achieved. They are motivated to have, get, achieve, attain, and so on. Because of their concentration on goals to be accomplished, they tend to be good at managing priorities. Moreover, they are excited and energized by their goals.

They often have trouble either recognizing what should be avoided, or identifying problems. At the extreme, they are perceived as naive by others because they do not take potential obstacles into account.

Away From

People who have an Away From pattern notice what should be avoided and gotten rid of, and otherwise not happen. Their motivation is triggered when there is a problem to be solved or when there is something to move away from. They are energized by threats. A salesperson told me: "If I don't get out there and sell, I won't be able to pay my bills at the end of the month." Deadlines, for example, get these people into action. People with an Away From pattern in a given Context are good at troubleshooting, solving problems, and pinpointing possible obstacles during planning, because they automatically pick up on what is or could be going wrong.

They may have trouble maintaining focus on their goals because they are easily distracted by and compelled to respond to negative situations. This is the kind of person who will drop everything to fix something. At the extreme they forget what the priorities are and only concentrate on treating crises. If this person is at the top of a department or an organization, the *entire organization will be run by crisis management.* Away From people have some difficulty managing priorities because whatever is wrong will attract most of their attention. People who have a strong Away From orientation in a given Context are often perceived as jaded or cynical, particularly by Toward people.

Distribution _____ %

(*in the work Context, from Rodger Bailey*)

Toward	Equally Toward & Away From	Away From
40%	20%	40%

Most people will have a mainly Toward or mainly Away From pattern on this continuum, in a given Context.

Pattern Recognition
≈≈≈

Questions

WHY IS HAVING THAT (THEIR CRITERIA) IMPORTANT?

or

WHAT WILL HAVING THAT (THEIR CRITERIA) DO FOR YOU?

Toward—sentence structure
• talks about what they gain, achieve, get, have etc.
• inclusion
• what they want, goals

Toward—body language
• pointing toward something, head nodding, gestures of inclusion

Away from—sentence structure
• will mention situations to be avoided, gotten rid of
• exclusion of unwanted situations, things
• problems

Away from—body language
- gestures of exclusion, shaking head, arms indicating that something is to be avoided, gotten rid of

Note: Listen to what a person says after the word **because**. It will either be a Toward or an Away From statement.

Examples

Toward:	"I would get personal satisfaction and a promotion."
Mainly Toward:	"I would get a promotion, personal satisfaction, make more money and not have to go on the road."
Equally Toward and Away From:	"I would get personal satisfaction and not have to go on the road."
Mainly Away From:	"I would not have all this routine work, or be away from my family often, plus I would get a promotion."
Away From:	"I would get away from this boring work, all the deadlines, and my boss who keeps looking over my shoulder."

You will need to ask the questions in a series or laddering approach, as follows:

SRC:	Adam, can you give me your Criteria for a job?
A:	Effective, more proficient, fun and taken seriously.
SRC:	All right, Adam, *why is having that important?*
A:	To help people.
SRC:	To help people. And why is that important?
A:	Because I get satisfaction from helping people.
SRC:	So why is satisfaction important?
A:	Well, *that's what I want* from a job.

Here's a different example:

SRC:	Joanne, what do you want in a job?
J:	I like to know what I have to do, and to be evaluated based on my own performance.
SRC:	Why is that important?
J:	It gives me a sense of calm.
SRC:	And why is *that* important?
J:	If I'm not calm with myself, I can't be calm with my kids.
SRC:	And why is that important?
J:	*It keeps me from hitting my kids.*

Joanne wanted to have her Criteria met in order to prevent a certain outcome, while Adam was motivated to attain his Criteria in order to achieve an outcome.

The reason we ask the Motivation Direction questions several times is to get a more accurate sense of where the person puts their energy: *toward goals* or *away from* problems. In my experience, when we ask the question only once, we often get a one-line Toward answer, regardless of the person's actual pattern. I believe that is because many of us have subscribed to the "Power of Positive Thinking," and so devalue the importance of recognizing problems.

There was an elderly gentleman who resided at a hotel. Every evening he shuffled gingerly to the front desk to get his keys and over to the elevator to go up to his room. One day he got his keys and went up the elevator as usual, only to immediately return to the front desk. He addressed the clerk: "Young lady, I have a problem." The bright young employee had been trained in customer service and the power of positive thinking, so she replied: "We don't have problems here, sir, we have challenges!" The gentleman snorted and said: "Harumph! I don't know if it's a problem or a challenge, but there is a woman in my room."

So we ask the questions about three times to find out what is behind the answer, or what is triggering the person into action in that Context.

Alternate Questions:
> What's the point?
> Why bother?
> What's important about X?
> What's in that for you?

So, Why *Did* You Leave Your Last Job?

Changes in Context

Why *did* you leave your last job? Because you couldn't stand it anymore? Or because there was something better on the burner? Why did you leave your last spouse? Because you were unhappy, or because there was someone else on the horizon? Why did you take your last vacation? Was it because you wanted a break from the grind or because you were interested in doing something in particular?

You may have a Toward pattern in one Context and an Away From pattern in another Context.

Can your Direction change over time? Yes, it can. Your response to a single significant event may change your pattern. Let's say someone has a Toward pattern and has all kinds of habits that probably are not good for his health. Then he has a heart attack and what happens? Because the heart attack was a very nasty yet compelling experience, he may change Direction and begin moving *away from* health problems. He might change his behaviour, quitting smoking, doing more exercise, changing his diet, and so on, because he *does not want* to have another heart attack. Some addiction treatment programs work on that basis.

Sometimes people do not make changes in their lives because they have not yet hit rock bottom. A helpful question to ask might be: "Do you *feel bad enough now* to make some changes or would you rather wait until you feel *even worse?*"

Influencing Language

Using the Influencing Language appropriately will get you a person's complete attention. That will prevent you from having to repeat things several times. The rapport that you establish will be deeper because you have matched how the person thinks; you will not have to spend a lot of time to get on the same wavelength. Because you have established rapport, you can avoid a lot of misunderstandings.

Here are some typical expressions to use:

Toward
- attain; obtain; have; get; include; achieve; enable you to; benefits; advantages; here's what you would accomplish

Away From
- won't have to; solve; prevent; avoid; fix; prevent; not have to deal with; get rid of; it's not perfect; let's find out what's wrong; there'll be no problems

What Would Make You Set and Attain Goals?

For many years people have been teaching and learning about the importance of setting goals. It has been proven many times that if you do not have goals, chances are you will not be able to find what you truly want. Was that last sentence a Toward statement or an Away From statement? It was Away From. You don't get anywhere if you don't have goals.

When we are discussing a person's Motivation Direction, we are talking about what will **trigger** her into doing something, such as setting goals. Why do I personally set goals in my business? Because if I didn't, I would be totally disorganized. I do set goals, and I have an Away From pattern at work. For me, this means that I can get distracted by whatever squeaks the loudest. In order to stay focused on what I am to achieve (and particularly so as *not* to become disorganized), about every two weeks I ask myself: "What business am I in?" This helps me recenter on what I really need to be doing. Another useful question for Away From people to ask themselves is: "How does this activity fit in with what I want to accomplish?"

Toward people need to ask themselves: Are my plans going to work? What else do I need to predict? What haven't I thought of yet that may go wrong? They may need the services of a devil's advocate in order to make sure they are being realistic.

While North American culture seems to have a bias against the Away From pattern, there is a need for a balance between Toward and Away From in many situations. A good equilibrium between Toward and Away From on a team will help ensure that goals are set, well-laid contingency plans are made, and focus is kept on priorities.

Is It Fear of Success or Motivation Direction?

Here's another consideration regarding Away From people and goal achievement. Let me give you an example. This happened to John Overdurf, a therapist I know. He had a client who came to see him and said: "I'm very upset. My life is really going down the tubes. I've been a millionaire four times." At first glance you might say, "You've been a millionaire four times. So what's the problem?" Let's think about it. If he has been a millionaire four times, that means he lost it three times. So let's look at what happened.

John asked him some questions and found out that he had an extreme Away From pattern about work. He was motivated *to move away from poverty*. Let's put this on a graph to understand his pattern. On the vertical axis, we have his amount of motivation, or how motivated he is, from "not very motivated" at the bottom to "very motivated" at the top. Let's put revenue on the horizontal axis, zero revenue to one million dollars. If he is highly motivated away from poverty, at zero revenue, how motivated is he? Very motivated. As he earns money, what happens? His interest level declines as his revenue increases. Once poverty was not an issue, he would not finish work on contracts, or he would forget to submit quotes to potential clients, or procrastinate and not follow up. When the big contract would come that could push him over the million-dollar point, he says "Ahh, I'll do it when I get around to it," whereas when he is threatened by poverty (whatever that means to him) he is highly motivated to do whatever it takes to generate revenue.

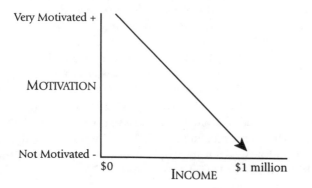

Although this is an extreme example, it explains why highly Away From people need to recenter at regular intervals on what they are trying to achieve.

Positive or Negative Thinking?

When first acquainted with these patterns, many people judge people with a Toward pattern as positive, while the Away From pattern is seen as negative. This judgment comes from a certain interpretation of the words "positive thinking." Remember that these patterns are simply triggers that will catapult someone into action.

Mother Teresa was quoted as saying that she started her work when "I discovered there was a Hitler in my heart." Her Motivation Direction is Away From. Many lobby groups, such as Greenpeace, the National Action Committee for the Status of Women (NAC), the anti-nuclear movement, Amnesty International, and so on, are essentially motivated to move away from certain practices with which they do not agree. You can therefore predict that these groups will notice what is insufficient or wrong with government legislation to protect the environment, rape victim protection laws, nuclear safety regulations, welfare reform, and so on. Many journalists also have this pattern.

Here is a statement by Nelson Mandela, on May 24, 1994, the day he became President of South Africa:

> *"My government's commitment to create a people-centred society of liberty binds us to the pursuit of the goals of . . .*

(at first glance this sounds pretty Toward, doesn't it?)

> *freedom from hunger, freedom from deprivation, freedom from ignorance, freedom from suppression and freedom from fear."*

If a person answers "freedom" in response to *Why is that important?*, do not assume that it is either Toward or Away From. Probe to find out if it is freedom *to* or freedom *from*.

Conflicts of Language in Labour Relations

In the Context of labour relations and negotiations, conflict arises not only because of the often contrary vested interests of labour and management. Conflict also arises because of the cultural differences between the two groups. If I can make a generalization for a moment, let's take top management as a culture. Is top management mainly Toward or Away From? Goals, business plans, objectives, and so on, are Toward activities. What is the primary reason for the existence of a union? To make another generalization, unions often exist to protect their members from disasters: poor pay, bad working conditions, lay offs, and the like.

Frequently management and labour do not speak the same language. Management tends to negotiate in terms of moving toward its objectives, while labour attempts to prevent certain things from occurring.

In 1995 the Canadian rail strike/lockout between the Canadian National Railway (CN) and the Canadian Pacific Railway (CP) on the one hand, and the Canadian Auto Workers (CAW) and the Brotherhood of Maintenance of Way Employees (BMWE) on the other, gave clear examples of these patterns at work. The principal issue was over employment security, a hard-won benefit that the unions were determined to *prevent* the railways from changing, particularly in the face of possible privatization of CN and massive layoffs. The railways were equally determined to modify the contract in order to *increase* their competitiveness with American railways and the trucking industry. In this example, each side was moving in a different Direction and, as is the case in labour disputes that escalate, operating out of different Criteria.

If labour and management could each learn to understand the patterns of the other side, and learn how to speak in their language, they would improve their chances of reaching agreement with less strife.[2] Of course, in Reality, not all unions have an Away From motivation, nor do all employers have a Toward pattern.

Professions Have Cultures

Some professions are inherently Toward or Away From. For example, medicine, as it is usually practised in the West, is highly Away From. As a culture (as distinct from individual patterns) medical practitioners tend to focus on what is wrong with their patients. They move *away from sickness and dying.* I recently completed profiling all the pharmacists in a hospital and found that, out of seventeen pharmacists, fourteen had a mainly or highly Away From pattern at work. The other three were only slightly on the Toward side of the equation. As a culture, the medical professions are so Away From, that when the idea occurred to them that holistic health might be something worth considering, they called it *Preventative Medicine.*

The Away From orientation is appropriate for treating and curing (getting rid of) disease. Can you imagine rushing in to your doctor about a medical emergency, and when you see her, she ignores your symptoms only to ask you about your health goals?

On the other hand, a number of medical practitioners work outside the traditional medical structures. I am willing to bet that many herbalists, iridologists, and others have a Toward pattern about their work and

---

2. For much more complete information on how to negotiate, please see Fischer and Ury's **Getting to Yes**, Ury's **Getting Beyond No**, and Fischer's **Beyond Machiavelli**.

do not feel comfortable with people who primarily seek out and destroy disease.

As you read about the different patterns, you may find that you can deduce the cultural patterns of different professions.

Hiring

If you are going to hire someone, it would be useful to know whether the day-to-day activities of the job consist mainly of troubleshooting and problem-solving or rather concentrating on the attainment of objectives. Although most organizations are now, at the very least, paying lip service to performance appraisals based on employee objectives, you will need to examine the day-to-day realities of the position more closely.

To assist a design and manufacturing firm in hiring a plant manager, I needed a list of responsibilities and tasks that this person would perform. The tasks included monitoring production reports and investigating causes of errors in production, shipping, and data entry; ensuring that shipments are properly done; quality control; government compliance; negotiating with suppliers and facility maintenance. With the possible exception of negotiating with suppliers, most of the activities needed to meet these responsibilities required looking for, preventing, and solving problems. A Toward Plant Manager would have missed many of the potential errors and omissions while charging ahead to meet production targets. (I have noticed that many people who have an Away From pattern call targets "deadlines.") I also profiled the senior management to ensure there would be a balance in the team, and someone would be looking out to make sure objectives were met.

If you want to hire someone motivated to perform the job at hand, it is important to determine whether the job is goal-oriented or is mainly troubleshooting. Do you need someone who is excited about working toward goals, or someone who delights in solving crises?

I will deal with how to write career advertisements to only attract the "right" candidates in the Applications section of the book.

People Management and Task Assignment: The Carrot or the Stick

Since most managers already have a team of existing employees, they would be well advised to discover what their strengths are, and to capitalize on those strengths instead of suffering from the weaknesses.

To get and keep Toward employees motivated, they will need tasks that allow them to attain goals. You can tell them the benefits of doing a certain task, such as *improving* efficiency, *increasing* departmental revenue, or *receiving a bonus*. In meetings they will want to stay focused on the objective and will have little patience for discussions about what might go or is going wrong. They will consider such talk as off-topic. You will need to explain to them the benefits of discussing potential problems and make sure you do

that in Toward terms: "If we discuss and plan for potential problems now we'll reach the objective that much sooner," is more appropriate than: "If we don't look at problems now, we'll be unprepared later."

Toward employees, particularly when they also have a Proactive pattern, if left to charge on to their goals, may get some nasty surprises later, due to inattention to potential hurdles or unforeseen negative consequences.

Away From employees will steer meetings into discussions of obstacles and what is wrong with proposals. To help them be most productive in meetings, explain to them (in Away From terms) why keeping the goal in mind will *prevent the group from losing focus,* which could be a major *waste of resources* and allot them time for *disaster prevention.* For tasks, give them problems to solve and things to fix. Impending disaster will energize them. "If this isn't out on time, they'll have our heads." The worst thing that you, as a manager, could do to an Away From employee is to take away all their problems. "Nothing's wrong, I'm worried." You, as a manager, also may not want to cope with the results of giving a Toward task to an Away From employee.

I also suggest that you do not ask a Toward employee to proofread a document. They will not pick out the errors. If you notice mistakes in text as if they jumped out of the page, then you have an Away From pattern in the Context of reading. I gave the first draft of this book to a friend to read over, having forgotten about her Toward pattern. Apart from adding a couple of commas, she said, "It's just great," and went on to tell me all the things she liked about it.

The Cure to Writers' Block

When you write letters, reports, articles, or books, do you ever suffer from Writer's Block? If this happens regularly, then you probably have an Away From pattern in this Context. It is much easier, and more motivating, for Away From people to correct mistakes than it is for them to remain focused on the goal of their text.

My philosophy is to work from my strengths, as opposed to suffering from my weaknesses. So, knowing about my Away From pattern, I decided to write this book by doing what I do best: fixing what's there. To do this, I had my audio tape series on the same topic transcribed and put onto diskette. Then I structured the book and imported sections of the transcript. Lastly, I did the fun part. I corrected the text, turning spoken language into written text, looking for errors and omissions, needed updates, and new examples.

I told my sister-in-law, who is a writer, that I was able to produce about twenty-two pages of text per day. She found this to be incredible until I explained that: "I wasn't writing twenty-two pages, I was correcting twenty-two pages and adding in what was missing."

My advice to those of you who suffer from Writer's Block is to get *anything* down on paper (or up on the screen), even if you have to ask someone

A very Toward dog!

else to draft a letter, for example. Then fix it. It will be much less tedious and you won't waste a lot of time wondering what to say.

Of course this trick would not help you if you *really* had nothing to say.

Sales and Marketing

Just out of curiosity, I phoned the local Automobile Association, and asked: "Why do people buy your service?" They told me that 90 percent of their members join the club to avoid problems such as having their car break down and paying a fortune for a tow. In the Context of travel by car, the vast majority of their members therefore have an Away From pattern.

I recently had the opportunity to work with the Automobile Association. To explain what I meant by Toward and Away From, I took the management down to the front desk to eavesdrop on what customers were saying. Person after person said that they *didn't want to have to deal with* breakdown problems, expensive alternatives, and so on. As a result we redesigned their marketing, sales, and customer service processes to use mainly Away From language: "Your one-stop worry-free travel agency," "You won't have to deal with . . . ," "You needn't worry about . . . ," "No-fee travellers cheques," "This will save you time," and the like.

Insurance is another Away From product. Most customers buy to avoid problems for themselves or their families. Investments, on the other hand, are inherently Toward. Imagine the difficulty insurance sales people must have had when insurance companies also began offering investment opportunities. They would have had to get their insurance customers into Toward thinking. Often they merely continued the pattern, pointing out the financial disasters inherent in not investing wisely.

I assisted the marketing department of a major pharmaceutical manufacturer in profiling its market. We also reviewed its print advertisements in light of our findings. One of their ads for a drug to prevent urinary incontinence had been particularly successful. It showed a smiling man in his sixties, swinging a golf club on a beautiful sunny day. The caption read: "18 holes and no accidents." Until we had diagnosed the Profile, they had assumed that the ad worked because of the positive scene in the picture. After they understood the nature of the product and the market in Away From terms, it was agreed that it was the caption that created the positive response.

As a salesperson or marketing director, there are several options you could take when planning your sales approach or marketing campaign. You can examine your product or service to discover if it is Toward or Away From by its very nature, and design your process to attract more of the appropriate market segment. Alternatively, especially if your product or service could be both, you could design your strategy to adapt to either, based on your individual customer's triggers. Another option is simply to find out who is already buying your product or service regardless of the characteristics of the product, and gear everything to increase your market share within that group. Or, if you have already saturated that group, you may judge it appropriate to go after the other pattern by using the correct Influencing Language.

Many books on sales will tell you that a person will buy either to *gain a benefit* or to *avoid a problem*. Once you have asked the question *Why is that important?*, to determine a Toward or Away From motivation, you can use the appropriate Influencing Language. If you want to sell a house to a Toward family, you might tell them (if it matches their Criteria) that this house *is close* to the schools, *has lots* of room, and *is near* public transport. For an Away From family, you could say that it *isn't far* from the schools, *isn't too small*, and you *don't have to walk miles* to get to public transport.

One real estate agent who studied and used the LAB Profile found that he only had to work two-thirds of the year to keep his income at the level he wanted, and this during a recessionary period when many agents had been forced to leave the business.

Culture

The LAB Profile is a tool that will enable you to understand cultures, corporate or national. One of the questions that has preoccupied Canadians for many years is: "How specifically are we different from Americans?" America, as a culture, is Toward. (Remember that *culture* is an umbrella; any given individual may or may not fall under that umbrella.) In Europe, Americans are perceived as extremely naive, because they just go ahead and do things, disregarding the possible negative implications. While I was living in France during the 1980s, I did some training and consulting for the OECD (The Organization for Economic Co-operation and Development) and UNESCO (The United Nations Educational, Scientific, and Cultural Organization). The criticism I heard many times about the Americans within those organizations was that "They always think that just because it's a good idea, we should go ahead and do it. They don't seem to understand that there is this political consideration and that possible problem, etc." You may recall that the American government withdrew from UNESCO.

Canadians, on the other hand, have a more Away From pattern, as a culture. We do not want to rock the boat or create waves. And look at my own Jewish culture. Any group that posts a slogan of "Never Again" and prescribes chicken soup because "it couldn't hurt" has to have an Away From pattern.

Summary

≋

Direction

Question: Why is that (Criteria) important? [Ask 3 times]

Toward: Motivated to achieve or attain goals.
Away From: Motivated to solve or avoid problems.
Distribution: 40% mainly Away From
                         20% equally Toward and Away From
                         40% mainly Toward

Influencing Language
Toward: attain; obtain; have; get; include; achieve, etc.
Away From: avoid; prevent; eliminate; solve; get rid of, etc.

⌒he Margaret Thatchers of the World: Motivation Source

≋

> *Where does the person find motivation? In external sources, or in internal standards and beliefs?*

This category deals with the source of motivation, or in other words, its location. Where are judgments made, inside a person's body or from outside? These patterns affect how you make judgments and decisions. As you try them out, you will be able to decide how best to use them, and others will notice your increased effectiveness.

Here are the two patterns:

Internal

People with an Internal pattern in a given context provide their own motivation from within themselves. They decide about the quality of their work. They have difficulty accepting other people's opinions and outside direction. When they get negative feedback on work they feel has been well done, they will question the opinion or judge the person giving the feedback.

They are motivated to *gather information* from outside sources and then *they decide* about it, based on internal standards. Because they *take orders as information*, they can be hard to supervise. "My boss wants this out by Tuesday? That's interesting."

Since they do not need external praise, they tend not to give much feedback as managers.

Internal people hold standards somewhere within themselves, for the things that are important to them. Their motivation is triggered when they get to gather information from the outside, process it against their own standards, and make judgments about it.

External

External people need other people's opinions, outside direction, and feedback from external sources to stay motivated. In the Context of work, if they do not get that feedback, they will not know how well they are doing. They take information as orders. "He said the green paper matches the decor. I'd better go get some."

They are motivated when someone else decides. They have trouble starting or continuing an activity without outside feedback or results of some kind.

External people do not hold standards within themselves. They gather them from the outside. In the absence of external feedback, they will experience something akin to sensory deprivation.

Distribution _____ **%**

(*in the work Context, from Rodger Bailey*)

Internal	Equally Internal & External	External
40%	20%	40%

Pattern Recognition
≋

Question: HOW DO YOU KNOW THAT YOU HAVE DONE A GOOD JOB? (at work, at choosing a car, etc.)

Internal—sentence structure
- they decide or know themselves; "I know"
- they evaluate their own performance based on their own standards and Criteria
- they resist when someone tells them what to do, or decides for them
- outside instructions are taken as information

Internal—body language
- sitting upright, pointing to self, may pause before answering a judgment from someone else while they evaluate it, minimal gestures and facial expressions for their culture

External—sentence structure
- other people or external sources of information decide or judge for them
- need to compare their work to an external norm or standard i.e., a checklist or a quota
- outside information is taken as a decision or order

External—body language
- leaning forward, watching for your response, facial expressions indicating they want to know from you if it was all right

Examples

Internal:	"I know when I have done a good job."
Mainly Internal:	"I usually know. I appreciate it when my boss compliments me, but generally, I know when I have done well."
Equally Internal and External:	"Sometimes I know and sometimes my clients tell me."
Mainly External:	"Usually, when I meet the quotas set by my boss and my clients seem happy. And also I can tell when I am working well."
External:	"My clients are happy. My boss is happy. I met my quota."

Alternate Questions:

How would you react to regular feedback from peers in (a specific Context)?

Whom do you involve when you make a decision?

If you felt you had done good work and someone you respect criticized your work, how would you react? Listen if the person criticizes, judges, or attempts to persuade the other person (Internal), or if they question the value of their own work (External).

Questioning and testing:

Here are some examples to show you how to test if you are not sure from the answer to the first question:

SRC:	Can I ask you, Suzanne, how do you know you've done a good job at work?
S:	Feedback from other people plus knowing myself. (External & Internal)

This is an example of someone with both patterns. Because we know that only about 20 percent are right in the middle, I would like to test to see if Suzanne falls on one side or the other.

SRC:	Let's say you thought you did a good job on something and you didn't get good feedback from the other people. How would you react?
S:	Well, I'd still *think* I did a good job but . . . something would be missing. I'd have to go check what they didn't like.

Here are two more examples:

SRC:	Louise, how do you know you've done a good job at work?
L:	I feel good about it.
SRC:	What happens if you feel good about it and nobody else appreciated it?
L:	They probably didn't see what I saw in it (shrugging her shoulders).
SRC:	Robert, how do you know you've done a good job at work?
R:	I know I've done a good job when I get external feedback.
SRC:	What happens when there is no external feedback?
R:	I would feel, like, what's the point?

While Suzanne has both patterns at work, she has more External than Internal, because when push comes to shove, she needs the feedback to really know if it is good enough. Both Louise and Robert fall firmly in the Internal and External camps, respectively.

Where Do You Know That?

I recently discovered another question that will help you test in those cases where the answer to the first question is unclear. Ask: "*Where do you know that?*" An Internal person will point to a part of their body and an External person will either not understand the question or give a clear External answer.

Other Contexts

I have worked with many groups in which there are quite a few men with a highly Internal pattern. Often one of them will voice his conviction that he is always Internal because how else could one run one's life? I ask: "How do you know you bought the right house?" The answer frequently is: "Because my wife liked it."

Someone in a training group said to me, "Well it seems to me this External stuff is really immature. Obviously, when you grow up and gain a certain amount of maturity, you become more Internal." This is a typically Internal thing to say. Let's consider another possibility. Someone who has been highly Internal might define maturity as the ability to take other people seriously by responding to what they *say* they need, instead of *knowing* what is best for them. It depends on where you are coming from and what you are trying to achieve, whether it is more appropriate to be in an Internal mode or an External mode, or both.

Margaret Thatcher

When the Commonwealth countries were negotiating about whether to impose sanctions against South Africa during its long Apartheid period, the vote was forty-nine countries in favour of sanctions to one against. Who was the holdout? The United Kingdom. Who specifically? Margaret Thatcher. When the vote was announced, she declared: "I feel sorry for the other forty-nine." Margaret Thatcher has an *off-the-scale* Internal pattern.

Brian Mulroney, Michael Wilson, the GST, and Free Trade

I believe that the LAB Profile can help us understand what happened when the conservative government in Canada under Brian Mulroney brought in the very unpopular Goods and Services Tax (GST). Finance Minister Michael Wilson initiated the GST and originally announced in 1990 that it was to be levied at 9 percent. Who lowered it to 7 percent? The Prime Minister, Brian Mulroney. How could this happen? Wouldn't you suppose that when a finance minister announces a new tax, he has the support of the prime minister?

Michael Wilson has a strong Toward and Internal combination. He had calculated that in order to meet his goals he needed the GST to be set at 9 percent. The Canadian public vociferously rebelled at the thought of a new tax during a difficult economic period. And how did Michael Wilson respond? He expressed some regret that the public was upset but insisted that the 9 percent was needed to meet his targets.

When the fury escalated, Brian Mulroney intervened over Mr. Wilson's head and lowered the tax to 7 percent. Mr. Mulroney has a combination of Away From and External patterns, which means that he is motivated to respond to outside negative feedback. As Prime Minister he was well known for *governing by opinion poll*, jumping into action whenever specific groups yelled loud enough. (I suspect that President Clinton also has this pattern.)

This pattern combination also explains Mr. Mulroney's behaviour in the summer of 1992 regarding the negotiations on the Charlottetown Constitutional Accords. While Mr. Mulroney was away in Europe, the provincial premiers came to a preliminary agreement on a new federal system for the country, with former prime minister Joe Clark, who was representing the federal government. As a result of negative public reaction to the agreement, Brian Mulroney vetoed it upon his return to Canada.

Who oversaw the Canadian negotiations for the North American Free Trade Agreement (NAFTA)? Mr. Michael Wilson, who by this time had become the trade minister. With his combination of Internal and Toward, he neglected to foresee potential problems in the agreement, in spite of the warnings that came from both commentators and advocacy groups. An important omission in the final agreement was the creation of a fair and timely dispute resolution mechanism.

Since the agreement came into effect, there have been many long, drawn-out, high-level conflicts between Canadian and American producers of steel, softwood lumber, Durham wheat, and beer. I often wonder, if the Minister had been slightly less Internal and more Away From, whether some of these problems could have been avoided.

Making Criticism and Responding to Feedback

When an External person receives criticism or negative feedback, they question themselves. An Internal person in the same situation makes a judgment about the other person. "I must have done something wrong" (External) or "the customer is a jerk because he didn't appreciate what I did for him" (Internal).

If ten people say to a highly Internal person: "Boy, is your tie ugly!" he would say "Gee, isn't that funny? There are ten people walking around here with bad taste." An External person would go home and change.

I had the advantages of being External driven home to me recently. I bought a cheap bookcase, in a kit, which I had to assemble myself. As I was struggling to follow the instructions (my father used to say that if all else fails, read the instructions), I noticed that the top and bottom shelves did not fit properly onto the back board. "Cheap design," I grumbled to myself and I *made* it fit. When I set the bookcase up I noticed that I had assembled the top and bottom shelves backwards and the chipboard was showing! Had I been slightly more External, which is appropriate in Contexts one knows little about, I might have *questioned what I was doing* when I noticed the poor fit, instead of *criticizing the design*.

When following instructions, it may be more appropriate to be in an External mode. My twin brother confirmed this to me when we were discussing how the holes often seem to be in the wrong place in these sort of kits, that is, until you figure out that *you* made the mistake!

Recently when I returned to Paris to do some work, I went out to supper with a friend. She suggested a restaurant where she had liked both the food and the ambiance. "Although," she said," I've heard it's been taken over by new management, and that it's not nearly as good anymore." She then went on to insist that we go there anyway because she had to go see *for herself*. At the end of the evening she pronounced," Well, they were right; the service was poor and so was the food. But I had to check it out for myself." Because she was highly Internal, someone else's word was not good enough. It remained an unresolved issue for her until she could decide for herself.

Many women tell me that their husbands often do not believe them when they tell them that there is something wrong with the car. The husbands need to find out for themselves.

The easiest way to get an Internal person to listen and think about something is to phrase it as "information you might want to consider"; otherwise they may simply judge you or the way you said it.

Influencing Language

You might want to consider choosing your words carefully, based on the information you have gathered about someone. As the most skilled professional communicators can tell you, the impact will be enormous.

Internal
- only you can decide; you might consider; it's up to you; I suggest you think about; try it out and decide what you think; here's some information so you can decide; what do you think?; for all the information you need to decide, just call . . .

External
- you'll get good feedback; others will notice; it has been approved by; well-respected; you will make quite an impact; so-and-so thinks; I would strongly recommend; the experts say; give references; scientific studies show

What Self-Esteem Is Not

Someone asked me about these patterns. "Is it possible for a person to switch from Internal to External, or vice versa, depending on whether he or she receives positive or negative criticism?" As Rodger Bailey, the developer of the LAB Profile, said: The LAB Profile is a status report about how I (with my particular structural makeup) respond to Contexts." In a few of the profiles I have done, I noticed a pattern that corresponds to the question above. One person was highly Internal when she thought she had done a bad job (one Context) and highly External when she thought she had done something well (a different Context for her). Nothing anyone would say could convince her that she had done a good job when she had decided otherwise. However, when she thought she had done something well, she had to check with others to make sure it was all right. I suspect that this has to do with low self-esteem and self-confidence. I would this call it a self-handicapping strategy.

You should not, however, confuse an External pattern with low self-esteem. It is not the same thing. When I am presenting to a group, for example, where do I get my motivational energy? Do I get it because the participants are smiling at me, or because I know I prepared my presentation well? (In that Context, if my goal is to present well and meet the audience's needs, it is appropriate to do some of each.)

A friend of mine once asked me: "Do you think I'm too External?" She then realized what she had said and began to laugh. My response was: "Too

External for what?" I used to be influenced by peer pressure but my friends talked me out of it.

Educational Design

I was working with a large group of highschool principals in the province of New Brunswick and we were discussing the design of education programs. One of the participants made the comment that many of the new programs are structured to create an Internal pattern in the students. In my opinion, when you closely examine the structure and content of any educational program, you could probably do a LAB Profile of its creator. Most programs will favour one or the other pattern in each of the categories. The Principal's question was: "What about the kids who have an External pattern in school and therefore need outside feedback to stay motivated and to know if they are doing well?"

I believe that it is fine to teach and encourage self-evaluation. However, when you want to *trigger motivation and keep the students interested* (which is a separate Context), some people will need ongoing feedback or results to stay interested.

Hiring

Does the job need someone who must *provide their own motivation and judge for themselves* the quality of their work? Or does it need someone to *adapt what they are doing based on outside requirements*? Sales and reception positions, or any job where meeting someone else's needs is crucial, generally need someone with an External pattern. You would want to employ someone in these positions for whom feedback will determine what they do and how they behave. These people will need either to be closely supervised, or to have some external means of knowing if they are on track.

Many people-management positions require someone who has a mainly Internal pattern with some External. Managers make decisions and set standards. You would have to have standards inside your body somewhere to do that. Frequently people say, however, when their boss is extremely Internal, that he or she does not listen or respond to suggestions.

For sales or customer service positions, you would need someone with a good dose of External. In today's market, sales and customer service people must really care whether customers are happy. If a customer is not pleased with your product or service and your representative explains that it is because the customer is an idiot, it will not help you improve customer service. Customers have become much more Internal than they once were. They have high standards for value and service, and one bad experience is enough to turn them off.

One of the challenges that large Internal organizations now face is how to incorporate spontaneous customer feedback into improving product design and service. I often find myself making suggestions to the person behind the desk, who sighs and says he can't do anything about it.

However, one of the latest currents in sales concerns promoting the salesperson as a *long-term partner and consultant* to clients. If your sales representatives do consulting, that presupposes that they have some expertise to impart, for example, on technical issues and standards. The salesperson/consultant would therefore need to have some degree of Internal. You would not, however, want someone who has an overly Internal pattern, because ultimately their performance needs to be judged by the satisfaction of the client.

When you are profiling a job in preparation for hiring or selection, you will need to determine whether the person's success at the position is based on meeting their own standards or adapting to someone else's.

People Management

Internal people have trouble accepting being managed, and generally do not need praise to stay motivated. Their motivation comes from inside; they are self-starters. They need to make their own decisions and will do that even when they have not been given permission. They become demotivated when they do not get to decide anything. When you give them an instruction, they will consider that as a piece of information and then decide whether to follow it.

A friend recounted an intercultural incident between two people with an Internal pattern, an English manager and an American employee. The English boss told his employee: "I'd reconsider that if I were you," intending to communicate that he thought it was a bad idea and it should not be done. The American took him literally; he reconsidered, decided it *was* a good idea, and went ahead and did it, much to the annoyance of his boss.

When two or more Internal people are on a team, you can predict that they will have frequent arguments and conflicts because each will be operating from their own (usually unstated) internal standards (particularly if they also have an Away From pattern). They can work more successfully together when they first negotiate and explicitly agree upon the standards and measurements.

Employees with an Internal pattern work best with little supervision. You can assign them a task and give them "carte blanche" to see it through. Give them decisions to make and, in cases where you are not sure of their judgment, get agreement on the standards to be met first. Make sure you know their Criteria and attach them to the job to be done. "Here's a *challenge* for you."

When giving them instructions, preface them with "Only you can decide to . . . " or "Here is the information on this; the end goal is to achieve that. You get to decide the best way."

External employees will look to their manager for guidance and encouragement. You will need to be explicit about what you expect them to do, as they tend to interpret information as instructions. If you said to an External employee: "The order forms are now available," they would drop what they were doing and go get them.

In the absence of regular feedback, they will become demotivated and unsure of themselves. Where the manager is highly External, she may end up looking to the employees for approval. External employees need to have clear goals and some external means of knowing if they are on track, in the form of regular feedback sessions, checklists, quotas, or examples to follow.

Annual performance appraisals are insufficient feedback for people who have an External pattern. Many will work themselves into a lather before their performance appraisal, because they have no idea themselves of how well they have been performing.

When assigning a task to an External person, let them know how much it will be appreciated (if his or her Organization pattern is Person) or what the impact will be (if his or her Organization pattern is Thing).* "You will get lots of good feedback," or "This will make a noticeable difference to our work" are phrases you could use to get their interest. The tasks that will play to their strengths are those that demand that they adapt to and meet someone else's expectations, provided that those expectations are clear.

Irresistible Language: Managing Your Boss

Some people are extremely hard to influence or convince, *until you know how.* Let's take an example of someone, perhaps your boss, who has the following combination: Internal and Away From. Chances are that this person has been making your life miserable by only noticing what you do wrong, and disagreeing with every proposal. As Groucho Marx sang, "Whatever it is, I'm against it."

So you need some *irresistible* Influencing Language, tailor-made for this person. Let's imagine that one day you enter her office with the report she asked you for and you say: "I've drafted the proposal you asked for to deal with the issues. *It's not perfect. Would you take a look at it?*" Your boss will grab the paper from your hand, correct it to her liking, and accept it.

Selling in a Buyer's Market:
Adapting to the Shift in Customers

As any business person will tell you, customers have become very difficult to deal with. They now demand products of perfect quality, resist complicated purchasing processes, and want anything that breaks to be fixed immediately at no cost to them. They quickly jump on any mistakes made, give customer service staff a very hard time, and even play one supplier off another to get the best deal. And they want more for less.

Guess what this means. The great customer shift has happened. Customers have become highly Internal to their suppliers. Suppliers beware!

---

*For more information on Organization, Person, and Thing, please refer to pages 123-128.

Spending time and money developing the best products and services for your clients may no longer be enough. You will also need to adapt your language and processes to meet the needs of people who take everything you say only as information to consider. Notice the skepticism with which clients scoff at your claims to be the best. "Prove it," they insist (to *their* satisfaction).

Canada Trust (a Canadian trust and mortgage company) seems to have responded to the change in the mortgage market. While once upon a time consumers would pay any interest rate just to get their mortgage accepted, since the early 1990s mortgage companies have had to beg people to choose them over the competition. The Canada Trust slogan was highly appropriate: "The best mortgage package in Canada? You be the judge."

When discussing sales and marketing, there are two axes to consider: promoting *who you are* (your organization's image or how you are perceived) and communicating to *the people you want to reach*. It is no secret that IBM, for example, has been struggling to be viewed as a more External company. They want to be perceived as giving the customer what the customer wants instead of what *they* have to offer. Their 1994 television commercial says it all: "We're trying to be more customer-focused." Trying?

You will need to decide what kind of image you want to convey. Are you the *experts* with the solutions or the company who will do whatever it takes to *meet your customers' needs*, or both?

Burger King has also been targeting Internals (and Proactives): "Your way. Right away." McDonald's, on the other hand, decides for you what you will have on your hamburger. If you do not believe me, try ordering a hamburger without mustard for your child at McDonald's.

The sales approach of a local career-counselling outfit consisted of booking an appointment with prospective clients, showing them the process they use, and then sending the person away to think about it and decide if they needed it. Upon questioning, it turned out that about 80 percent of their clients had an Internal pattern; so did the founder and majority of staff. When I suggested that they *might consider* using an approach for External people to attract more clients, the founder thought about it and decided against it. He felt that External clients would take up too much time in counselling sessions.

The national marketing director of a company that sells blood analysis equipment to hospitals spoke to me about a change in the buying process of their customers. Laboratory equipment used to be selected by the chief lab technician, who usually had a long-standing rapport with the sales representative. Now, all buying decisions are made centrally in the hospital purchasing department. The sales reps were finding themselves confronting highly Internal purchasing officers whose Criteria were about price and who did not understand the technical aspects of the equipment. They needed to change their sales approach by matching the price Criterion, giving only relevant information (one piece of which was the approval of the equipment by the chief lab technician), and asking the purchasing officer "to be the judge."

To sell to people who have an Internal pattern, you need to give them information and let them decide. I wrote an advertisement for a management training course geared to Internals with this statement at the bottom of the ad: "For all the information you need to decide, call. . . . " We had one person sign up over the phone without even bothering to find out what was in the course. We also had many calls for information that subsequently led to enrollments.

"I would like you to try it out and tell me what you think. The only way to know if this is the one for you is to test it out for yourself." That is why car dealerships insist that their sales people get the prospective buyer behind the wheel.

Doctors and Patients

In France I read a study that pronounced that 80 percent of patients do not finish taking their prescriptions. Doctors have told me that about the same percentage applies in North America. Many people simply forget to take their medicine when their symptoms disappear. We can use the LAB Profile to explain this. Many people have Internal and Away From patterns in the Context of bodily ailments. We tend to go to the doctor when we *feel* sick, not when someone else says we look unwell.

Doctors would therefore need to sell their patients on complying with their instructions. *"You need to decide* if you want to *get rid of this illness.* If you do, you will need to take all of this medicine, as prescribed" (Internal and Away From). Even though many people are External to doctors and other authority figures, once they get home they shift back into an Internal mode.

I believe that doctors need to recognize the implications of the fact that many of their patients shift into a highly External pattern in the doctor's office. Patients tend to believe whatever the doctor tells them because they have accepted the doctor as a knowledgeable authority figure. This means that doctors need to be very careful about what they say and imply.

My mother broke her wrist during an icy winter. I took her back to the hospital to have her cast replaced because the first one was too tight. The doctor fitted her new cast on and made a joke: "There, that'll keep you for *this time.*" This time?! Right before my eyes I watched my mother nod to acknowledge the implicit presupposition that if he was talking about *this time,* there was going to be a *next time!* "No!" I shouted, "This is the last time!" But my mother does not have an External pattern to me; I am her daughter. Three months later, she tripped in her garden and broke the other wrist.

Just to contradict what I said above, there is also another trend in the doctor-patient relationship. Millions of people are now consulting practitioners of complementary medicine. When asked why, many say either that the doctor has not been able to cure a particular problem or that they do not believe the approach used by the doctor can help them. These people have developed Internal standards for what they want and don't want.

Selling in Other Contexts

The approach for getting patients to take their medicine could also work for Internals in other Contexts. "You need to decide if you really want *(customer's desired outcome)*. If you do, then you'll need to try out *(our product or service)*."

External people need references. They need to know who else has bought. The advertisements where a famous person is flogging a product attract the attention of people who are External to that famous person, in that Context.

It can be easier selling to people provided you can get them to be External to you. This entails establishing credibility as well as rapport. One client of mine asked me: "Do you think I need it?" You can also do this by wearing clothes that are one notch more formal than your client's, showing credentials and references, and slipping in expressions such as "In my experience" or "If I were you, knowing what I know today . . . "

External people will also buy something for how it will make them look or the impact it will have on others. Why *do* people buy Jaguars? Because the leather seats are comfortable? A market researcher who worked on the Jaguar account told me that people today buy luxury cars more for the perceived value these cars offer than the status they confer. Then he stopped and thought. "Maybe," he snorted, "they are buying because they want to *be seen* as buying for value."

If you want to attract both groups, or if your client pays attention to both Internal standards and External feedback, use both patterns. For those cases where you are not sure, use one pattern and observe. If you do not get a positive response, try the other one.

Summary

≋

Source

Question: How do you know that you have done a good job at . . . ?

Internal: They are motivated to decide based on their own internal standards.

External: They need outside feedback to know how well they are doing and to stay motivated.

Distribution: 40% mainly Internal
20% equally Internal and External
40% mainly External

Influencing Language

Internal: only you can decide; you might want to consider; it's up to you; what do you think?, etc.

External: others will notice; the feedback you'll get; results; give references; so-and-so thinks, etc.

Sometimes You Just Gotta Break the Rules: Motivation Reason

> *How does a person reason? Is there a continual quest to find alternatives, or is there a preference to follow established procedures?*

This category will lead you to unlimited possibilities and show you the right way to get there. There are two patterns:

Options

People with an Options pattern in a given Context are motivated by opportunities and possibilities to do something in a different way. There is always another better way to do things. They love to create procedures and systems but have great difficulty following them. If you give an Options person a guaranteed way to make a million dollars, he will try to improve it.

They are thrilled by unlimited possibilities and ideas. The thing that is irresistible to Options people is breaking or bending the rules.

Options people like to start a new idea or a new project. However, they do not necessarily feel compelled to finish it. They much prefer to do development and setup rather than maintenance activities. Sometimes they will have difficulty committing themselves because they believe this will reduce their options. At the extreme, they might avoid deciding anything (particularly if they also have a Reactive pattern). Alternatively, they can be totally committed to an idea or project, until the next new idea comes along.

Procedures

People with a Procedures pattern like to follow set ways. They believe there is a "right" way to do things. Once they have a procedure they can follow it over and over again. These are people who are interested in *how* to do things, not in *why* things are the way they are.

A procedure has a beginning and an end. It may have choice points at which you gather more information and make a decision. Without one, Procedures people feel lost or get stuck. When they commence a procedure, the most important thing for them is to get to the end of the procedure. They are the ones who will complete and finish what they start.

They can feel personally violated when it is suggested to them to break, or go around, the rules. Once they know the procedure to follow, they are happy doing that.

Distribution _____ %

(in the work Context, from Rodger Bailey)

Options	Equally Options & Procedures	Procedures
40%	20%	40%

Pattern Recognition
≋

Question: WHY DID YOU CHOOSE YOUR PRESENT JOB? *(or house, vacation, car, etc.)*

You may recall that in the introduction of this book we discussed Reality. In order for people to create their own models of reality, they use three processes called Deletion, Distortion, and Generalization. This category deals with Distortion. The question we ask for this pattern is: "Why did you choose . . . " and the rest refers to a particular Context.

For Options people, when they hear the question **Why did you choose?**, they hear the question **why** and give you a list of Criteria for their answer.

When Procedures people hear the question, they delete the word **why** and substitute **how did it come to be?** They answer the question: "How?" Sometimes, the first thing they will say is, "Well, I didn't choose." They will tell you a story or series of events that led them to getting the job. "I was working at my brother-in-law's and there was an opening in this other company at the time I finished a contract, so I took it."

Options
- list of Criteria
- opportunities, possibilities
- expanding options and choice

Procedures
- did not choose
- answers the question "why" by telling "how" it came to pass
- the facts, events leading to, a story

How you recognize someone who has an equally Options and Procedures pattern is interesting. They might tell you a story with Criteria imbedded in it. I happen to be quite in the middle on this pattern, and if someone asked me why I chose to set up my own company after I returned to Canada, I would say: "After I came back, I looked around for what to do, and became a partner in a small training company. After a while I became **dissatisfied**. And **being organized** is important to me. I realized that I could probably make **more money** in my own company, and **decrease expenses** and **be independent**. So I set up my company, Success Strategies." I have used both patterns in the answer.

Examples

Options:	"I thought it would be stimulating, interesting, and challenging."
Mainly Options:	"It was more interesting, and had more responsibility and better pay. A friend of mine told me about it."
Equally Options and Procedures:	"A friend told me about it and it looked more interesting."
Mainly Procedures:	"I had been with the same company ten years. A friend told me they were hiring in her company, so I applied and was hired. The job is more interesting and I make more money."
Procedures:	"I didn't really choose. I met my boss through my brother-in-law who worked with her. They needed a technician and I was just completing a contract."
Alternate Question:	What would your typical work day be like? (listen for Criteria or a set of procedures to be followed) Note: Make sure you ask "*Why* did you choose?" and not "*How* did you choose?"

Influencing Language

The possibilities are endless for finding the right thing to say.

Options

- opportunity; choice; break the rules just for you; another better way; unlimited possibilities; an alternative is; that's one way; here are the options; there has got to be a way; the sky's the limit

Procedures

- the right way; speak in procedures: first . . . then . . . after which . . . the last step; tried and true; reliable; how to use this; just follow the procedure; the procedure is; proven methodology

Hiring

You can see that for hiring, the Options and Procedures patterns are quite important. In fact, this is one category where it really pays to get it right. When you profile a position, you will need to ask yourself whether the job mainly consists of *following procedures* or *creating and designing systems and procedures?* Is it setup and development, or maintenance? When you know what the balance is, you can write your advertisement to attract the right people and turn off the ones who would not fit. (See also the section on writing advertisements for jobs.)

You may have heard of some of the multilevel marketing companies or MLM's, such as NSA, Mary Kay, Nu Skin, and a number of other products. They have a real problem. Only one person in ten on average succeeds at making a full-time living at multilevel sales. I would say that this is very poor statistics for hiring, wouldn't you?

In my opinion, the reason is in how they promote themselves. The multilevel marketing companies try to recruit new distributors by telling them about *unlimited income possibilities.* This is Options language. Things with unlimited choice or possibilities, or no ceilings, or the sky's the limit, are *irresistible* to Options people.

However, when people actually become distributors they usually find that the companies have already worked out the procedures for selling the product. All you have to do is proactively and consistently follow the procedure to make your *sky's the limit* income, which most of them are incapable of doing. The irony is that if they used Procedures Influencing Language in their promotional packages, recruits would indeed make their unlimited income.

According to Rodger Bailey there has also been some research done on telemarketers, and this would apply to other kinds of salespeople. Telemarketers who have a Procedures pattern sell three times as much as the Options people. The reason for this is simple. Sales is basically a procedure. You contact prospective customers, establish rapport, do a needs analysis, present something that matches the needs, and lastly help the person make a decision. That's a procedure. If I am an Options person, this time I will do it one way; another time I will try another way. Options sales people tend to have an up-and-down performance, because occasionally they will get a brilliant idea and strike gold. They do not, however, hone their procedure until it works well. Procedures people will continue to follow the same process over and over again because it feels comfortable and right. This is ideal for sales (although in changing sales situations, they would need to be taught a new procedure).

Certain kinds of jobs are inherently Options or Procedures. Flying an airplane, for example, is quite clearly a procedure. Can you imagine a commercial airline pilot who has an Options pattern? "Let's go over the North

Pole this time." Anything to do with safety and security needs a Procedures person. Emergency procedures need to be memorized and followed to the letter. Someone who is Internal and Procedures would do very well at that kind of work. On the other hand, you would want an Options person to develop and test a safety procedure, preferably one who also has an Away From pattern to avoid mistakes.

Architecture would need someone with lots of Options and an understanding of Procedures. A building contractor would have a much heavier dose of Procedures to ensure compliance to regulations. You might want to test for this if you are going to do renovations.

Options people excel in situations where there is a need to develop creative solutions or alternatives to the present systems. Business process engineers, for example, would need a heavy dose of Options.

In a training company in France I worked closely with my boss, who has high Options and Internal patterns in his work. I learned much from him about creative seminar design. We frequently were asked to lead the same seminar several times over in the same large organizations. We would meet before each one to prepare and he would insist that we redesign each one. I would object: "But Pierre, it worked well last time, it was really good, and they liked it." He would say: "No, no, there has to be a better way to do this." I had the feeling we were constantly throwing the baby out with the bath water. You can see the conflict between Options and Procedures people.

In fact, to design training you need to develop Options, but in order to perfect the delivery of training you need to repeat enough Procedures to be able to reproduce processes that work. The best public speakers have well-honed routines, which necessitates doing both Options and Procedures.

For many years there has been a crisis in nursing; the media occasionally discuss examples from several European countries as well as North America. It is not solely attributed to low wages and abusive treatment by other medical professions. When I ask nurses: "Why did you choose to become a nurse?" the answer often is something like: "I want to help people," or "Once I got my certificate, I could travel." These are Criteria, Options answers. Many people attracted to nursing are interested because of the *possibilities* nursing has to offer. They are Options people. After they decide to become nurses, they go to nursing college. Who teaches in the nursing schools? People who did not find what they wanted in hospital work. So the nursing students get their certificates and go to work in the hospitals. What are hospitals all about? Procedures, and often very tight ones with little choice.

Now, in North America at least, where there is an increasing emphasis on home-based care, we have an expanding number of private nursing services. You can be a nurse, care for people, and do it your own way, getting a chance to develop alternatives. Hospitals themselves are also changing. One hospital I did some work for is well in advance of the trend in creating

A Little Variety

"Patient Care Teams," which include many of the medical professionals. This is a more Options approach to patient care.

To attract people who will perform well and be fulfilled by traditional hospital nursing, nursing educational institutions should be producing promotional materials that say: "Do you want to practice medicine the right way? Learn patient care from start to finish."

Culture Clashes at Work

One of the things I have noticed when participating in change operations in corporations is the internal culture clash between different departments. Let's take software design and marketing, for example. If you are a software designer, chances are you have a mainly Options pattern. You develop and design software. Marketing tends to be mainly Procedures because there are procedures to follow to take the product to market. The software designers develop some software and often they drop one project to work on another. They will keep changing it and adapting it and making it better and coming up with alternative solutions. The marketing department will be screaming at them: "Stop fixing it! Just give it to us so we can get it out on the market." Why are there so many upgrades to your favourite software package? A consultant friend summed up the software problem: "Not enough time to do it right once, but all the time in the world to fix it."

The same thing happens between the design engineers and the plant. What do design engineers do? They create systems and design products. What does the plant do? It makes them. Production managers get furious when engineering keeps changing the specs.

In order to work more effectively together and reduce the number of conflicts among Options and Procedures departments, each needs to understand the role of the other and how they function. Options people need to explore possibilities creatively in order to invent solutions. The Procedures people need to know that the fruit of these deliberations will actually arrive completed at the right time and place. Many companies would do well to have a person who handles Options and Procedures equally well to co-ordinate the work between these two departments.

Sales and Marketing

The means of choice for selling to an Options person is to get them to think of the possibilities. Give them lots of alternatives. They want to examine all the reasons *why* they should buy. I remember having a sales appointment with someone who was grappling with a problem. As I left, I inadvertently used an irresistible pattern. I said "There's gotta be a way to find what you're looking for." By the time I had returned to my office, the phone was ringing off the hook. She said: "You're right. There's gotta be a way. And you're the one who can help me." An Options person is motivated by unlimited choice. The more choice the better. To close the sale irresistibly, break with the normal procedure, just for them. My carpet cleaner told me: "The office says we have to charge $50 to clean the sofa, but since I'm already here, I can do that for you for $30."

If you want to know the right way to sell to a Procedures person, there are two keys. One is to get them started on a procedure because they are compelled to finish it, and the other one is to have them understand that this product or service is the tried and true, right way to do things. They will be more interested in *how* to buy it or use it than why they should buy it:

> *"The first step is, I'll show you the products. Then you can look at them. I will show you how to use them and you can try one out. You can then decide which one suits you best. After that, I'll tell you how the payment plan works and set it up for you to sign. Lastly, you can take your product home right away."*

You will have already started them on the first part of the procedure.

If the product meets their Criteria (and other factors do not interfere), they will complete the procedure. It is preferable to have the client going away happy with the product as the last step of the procedure, rather than paying the bill as the last step.

Certain kinds of stores naturally attract one or the other pattern. Some people (me, for example) are overwhelmed by the large amount of choice one has in music stores. Others are thrilled.

A well-known home furnishings chain that imports Far Eastern rattan furniture, cotton fabrics with Asian prints, and so on, ran an advertising campaign in magazines with an image on a grid pattern. A grid is a Procedures image. With this ad they increased their floor traffic by 20 percent. However, 75 percent of the people who walked in because of the ad, came into the store only once, and never came back. Why? It attracted Procedures people, but what does the store actually look like? It has clusters of stuff over here, clusters of stuff over there. It is very Options, lots of choice, all kinds of different materials, all kinds of gadgets, bricabrac, and so on. Bill Huckabee, a LAB Profile-trained market research consultant, looked at the results and designed a new advertisement. This time they laid out the ad in the same way the stores are laid out: clusters of images. They had another increase in store traffic, and a much higher percentage of the people who came in returned more than once.

Let's compare that chain to IKEA, the Swedish home furnishings put-it-together-yourself, store. When you walk into IKEA you cannot get out until you have gone through the entire store (short of pulling the fire alarm). I know; I have tried. They have a procedure for doing everything. They have procedures for walking through the store, measuring, deciding, ordering,

Terminal Options

The Latest Revision!

lining up, paying, parking, loading, and assembling the furniture once you get home.

Different Contexts create buying patterns among large groups of people. In the Context of buying cars, a large percentage of the population has an Options pattern concerning the car company and the model they choose. They might want a Ford Taurus or a Honda Civic, and they will tell you why. They are motivated by Criteria when they choose the make and model. Why did you choose your car? Because it has good fuel efficiency? Because it has great pick-up? Because there isn't another one like it on the road? Or some other Criteria? Probably not because you were walking along the street one day when you needed a car and happened to see one.

However, in the Context of choosing a dealership, most people have a Procedures pattern. This means they do not have Criteria about what dealership they choose. The first one they stumble on will do. For example, that is why all the Ford dealers in your region sponsor commercials together on local television stations. They know that which dealership you go to is of no importance, unless you experience very bad service and never want to go back there again.

Electronic marketing has grown by leaps and bounds over the last few years. There are many seminars that promote "exploring the sales opportunities of getting your company on the Internet" (Options language). Frankly, unless you have had your head in the sand since the mid-80s, you probably already know about the opportunities. I wish they would set up seminars to teach the step-by-step procedure for setting up web sites and so on.

Let's take fast-food chains again. When someone buys a McDonald's franchise, they find it is a turn-key operation. All the procedures are in place. The products are procedural as well. When you get a Big Mac it is always a Big Mac and it is always done the same way. The *right way.*

Compare them to Burger King one more time. Burger King's slogan in 1992 was: "Sometimes you just gotta break the rules." Now look at the Burger King products. You can have tomato or not, onions or not, relish and mustard or not, and so on. Options. Their 1993 slogan was: " Your way. Right Away." It is appealing to Proactive, Internal, Options people (in the Context of eating at fast-food places). I am willing to bet that their clientele has a different Profile from McDonald's. It has little to do with how their products taste. How different can one beef or chicken pattie be from another?

People Management

People with an Options pattern work best in situations where they get to develop or set up new systems and procedures. They will invariably find a way around standard operating procedures, so you will need to decide how best to harness their creativity. They will be motivated by tasks that involve creating something from scratch, particularly where the end result will increase options. To motivate them, you can tell them to think of the possibilities or to find an alternative to what we do now.

You can motivate Procedures people by telling them that this is the *right way* to do something. They feel comfortable doing the same thing over and over. Let them know how important the finished result is.

For staff who have both Options and Procedures patterns when at work, you will need to give them opportunities to both follow and develop or improve the procedures. You can use the Influencing Language for both patterns. "You will get to develop a better way to do this. Make sure it is right (Internal and Procedures), and then you can use it from now on." For someone who has an External pattern, you could substitute: "Check with me to make sure it is right. . . . "

Total Quality Management?

Many organizations have been preoccupied with introducing Total Quality Management, Continuous Improvement programs, and other forms of paradigm-shifting. They are aiming to get employees into new ways of thinking in order to respond to constantly changing environments. What are these programs designed to create? Options patterns. Basically the message is to tell workers that they ought to be Options people. You ought to be able to turn on a dime, totally change what you are doing, develop alternatives, and create new systems to anticipate and respond to changes.

What would actually happen to the corporate world, the helping professions, the education system, or any other sector, if no one finished or completed procedures? Imagine that for a moment. The new management practices have been designed to tell whole groups of people that what they do is no good, and yet if procedures were not completed, no money would be made.

I have found many biases against the idea of the Procedures pattern. My colleagues in France who teach the LAB profile found that they had to change the terminology. Instead of using the word *Procedures*, they changed it to *Process*. They found such a negative association with *being procedural* that people would not accept the term (and this in the country that invented the word *bureaucracy*).

I believe it is important to honour Procedures people for what they contribute, instead of pointing out to them how rigid this makes them. They get things done. We need Options people to think of new options, and we need Procedures people to see that they get done. Building a high-performance team depends on how well you use the different strengths in the team to accomplish what needs to be done.

Learning New Skills, or Why Some of Us Can't Understand Computer Nerds

Learning is a specific Context. People have different learning styles; knowing your Profile in that Context (or that of the people you are teaching) is useful for accelerating the speed at which new material can be integrated.

A few years ago I got my first computer. I had quite a few different packages of software with it. The person from whom I bought it was an experienced computer user, and he spent a lot of time teaching me. He would say, "I'd like you to *understand why* it's set up this way." I would say: "No, I don't want to understand why it's set up this way. Tell me *how* to turn it on." "Well," he would continue, "You need to *understand a few of the concepts* behind this particular program." "No I don't. I want to know *how you make* and *print* a document." Or he would say, in response to a how-to question: "There are *several ways* you can do this." And I would answer, feeling my blood pressure rise: "I don't want to know several ways. Just tell me *one way. The right way!*"

I needed the procedure to follow. It was only after I had mastered some needed procedures that I was the least bit interested in why things were set up the way they were. In that circumstance he could have matched my style by telling me: "I'm going to show you the *basic procedure* for making and printing a document. Once you've got that down, I'll explain *how it* works so that you can master the other things you'll need to do. Then *you will be able* to figure it out for yourself." An Options person would be motivated by all the possibilities the software has to offer. However, I suspect that many computer neophytes, and others learning new skills, simply want the procedure to follow.

Who writes the manuals for all your software and your computer? Options people, generally speaking. That is one possible explanation for why I, like many others, have difficulty understanding the manuals. The vocabulary is another problem. An exception is the very popular "For Dummies" series of manuals. They give you the step-by-step procedure and even warn you when they are about to give you some "technical drivel."

When you are learning or teaching something, it is useful to assess whether the need is to know the *why's* and *wherefore's*, or to simply know *how to*.

Working with Groups

When you are giving instructions to a group, if you give them options they will be paralyzed. You must be procedural when giving instructions to a group or they will not know what to do. I was giving an introductory workshop on the LAB Profile at a conference in Montreal and we did not finish all the patterns we wanted to do in the allotted time. The group seemed frustrated and wanted to continue. I said, "Okay, well there are some options. We could break for lunch now and come back early and do the last pattern, or we could keep going now and have lunch later, or we could just forget it. What would you prefer?" Everybody went um, ah, um. No answer.

I said "I have a suggestion. Let's break for lunch now. Those of you who want to, can come back a half an hour early and we'll meet in this room and we'll do it." They said great, and everyone left for lunch.

When explaining an exercise or assigning a task to a group, you need to give them explicitly the step-by-step procedure.

Coaching and Counselling

When we are coaching or counselling people, we often try to help them have more choice about what they do. If you have a Procedures person and you give him too many choices, you may inadvertently put him into sensory overload. Not deprivation, overload. Too much choice. What people with a Procedures pattern need is a procedure to enable them to discover what they want.

Summary
〰

Reason

Question: Why did you choose your current work (or house, etc.)?

Options:	Compelled to develop and create systems and procedures. Have difficulty following set procedures.
Procedures:	Prefer to follow tried-and-true set ways. Get stumped when they have no procedures to follow.
Distribution:	40% mainly Options
	20% equally Options and Procedures
	40% mainly Procedures
	in the Context of work, from Rodger Bailey

Influencing Language

Options:	opportunities; variety; unlimited possibilities; lots of choice; options; break the rules just for them
Procedures:	the right way; how to; tried and true; speak in procedures: first . . . then . . . lastly

---

When the Bell Tolls: Motivation Decision Factors

> *How does a person react to change and what frequency of change is needed? Does the motivation come from a search for "difference" or "sameness"?*

The Decision Factors category is about your internal time clock and how often the *bell rings* for change. Are you motivated by evolution, revolution, both, or stability? There are four patterns:

Sameness

People with a Sameness pattern want their situation in a given Context to stay the same. They do not like change and may refuse to adapt. They may accept a major change once every ten years, but they will provoke change only once every *fifteen to twenty-five years.*

Sameness with Exception

Sameness with Exception people like a given Context to stay mainly the same, but will accept change once a year if the change is not too drastic. They prefer their situations to evolve slowly over time. They tend to resist major changes except when they are perceived to be progressive or gradual. They need major change once every *five to seven years.* This is by far the largest category in the work Context, and probably in many other Contexts.

Difference

People with a Difference pattern love change; they thrive on it and want it to be constant and major. They will resist static or stable situations. They need drastic change about every *one to two years,* and if they do not get it, they may leave. They like change to be revolutionary, dramatically different.

Sameness with Exception and Difference (*the double pattern*)

People with this double pattern like change and revolutionary shifts but are also comfortable where things are evolving. They are happy with both revolution and evolution. They need major change every *three to four years*, on average.

Distribution _____ %

(*in the work Context, from Rodger Bailey*)

Sameness	Sameness with Exception	Difference	Sameness with Exception and Difference
5%	65%	20%	10%

Pattern Recognition
〰

Question: WHAT IS THE RELATIONSHIP BETWEEN YOUR WORK THIS YEAR AND LAST YEAR? (vacation, this home and the last one, etc.)

or

WHAT IS THE RELATIONSHIP BETWEEN THIS JOB AND YOUR LAST ONE?

The question asks: "What is the relationship between . . . ?" In this situation, the word *relationship* has the connotation of similarity. People will either naturally understand the word and tell you how it is the same or similar, or alternatively they will not know what you mean, or reinterpret it to mean how is it *different*.

Sameness
- how they are the same, identical
- what they have in common
- how it has not changed

Sameness with Exception
- how it has evolved over time
- it is the same except more; less; better; worse; improving; etc. (comparisons on a sliding scale)
- focus on the trip more than arriving at the destination

Difference
- may not understand the word *relationship*
- will describe how it is completely different

- new, different, changed, transformed, revolutionary
- language points to an immediate switch
- focus on the destination, ignore the trip

Difference and Sameness with Exception
- use *both* Difference and Sameness with Exception responses

Examples

Sameness:	"It is exactly the *same*. I'm *still* crunching numbers."
Sameness with Exception:	"It's the *same but* I have *more* responsibility and *less* time."
Difference:	"It's *totally different*. Now I do outside sales."
Difference and Sameness with Exception:	"There have been *big changes* this year and my performance has *improved greatly*."

To test your diagnosis in the work Context, simply ask the person how often they changed what they were doing on the job. They may have had the same job title, but what we are looking for is *how often* they changed responsibilities. Their answers will usually match the change clocks for their pattern. In other Contexts you could check by asking how often they have moved homes, what they do for a vacation each year, whether they go to the same cottage or do different things, and so on.

You will need to be especially clear in identifying the Context when you ask the question, because people's patterns often change depending upon what they are talking about. I profiled a man in several Contexts. Regarding work, he said, "Well it's *basically the same*: I have *more* responsibility, I've got *more* people to supervise, and *more* accounts." Sameness with Exception. Then I said, "OK, what's the relationship between the last holiday you took and the holiday before that?" He said "Relationship! What do you mean by relationship?" Two minutes after answering the first *relationship* question he was suddenly unable to understand the word *relationship*, simply because we had switched Contexts.

Influencing Language

Here are some totally new ways to improve communication and maintain rapport.

- **Sameness:** same as; in common; as you always do; like before; unchanged; as you already know; maintaining; totally the same; exactly as before; identical
- **Sameness with Exception:** more; better; less; the same except; advanced; upgrade; progression; gradual improvement; similar but even better; moving up; growth; improvement

- **Difference:** new; totally different; unlike anything else; unique; one of a kind; completely changed; unrecognizable; shift; switch; a complete turn around; brand new; unheard of; the only one
- **Sameness with Exception & Difference:** use both Sameness with Exception and Difference vocabulary

Making Your Change Pattern Work for You

Since people may have different patterns from Context to Context, it is important not to make generalizations about someone. A friend of mine, while he makes frequent changes in his work, always wants to go to the same restaurant to order the same thing. People who have a Difference pattern in the Context of reading usually have four or five books on the go at any one time. Some people have cottages where they spend their vacation every year; others would not consider going to the same place twice.

When I looked at my own history I discovered that I have moved residences about every eighteen months. I have also discovered that if you do that, banks and other financial institutions will think you are a flake. Guess what pattern they have?

Knowing your own pattern can help you to understand and predict what is happening in your life. When my change bell rang one fall, suddenly I started to notice all the things that were wrong with the place I was living. I was itching to move. I told myself that since I was working on a number of business projects and I needed co-operation from the bank, I would need them to perceive me as a steady, *normal* type. So I had my living room painted, bought some new furniture, moved around the old stuff, and made the whole place *feel different*. After I received the needed financial backing, I cracked and bought a new place.

I have a friend who has a combination of high Options and high Difference patterns in the Contexts of work and study. She started and had not completed three different Master's programs at three universities in different cities. She adopted three children from different backgrounds. After her first undergraduate degree, she went back to school and became a nurse. Every so often she would go back to hospital work because she really liked to take care of people. She would usually stay for a bit, get frustrated by the procedures, and leave. Her change pattern is an average of one to two years, and for some Contexts it is as short as six months.

As a student it was very difficult for her, because if she read a book once, she could not stand the idea of reading it again. She wanted to read something different. She did her Profile with me and decided, "I'm doing this Master's program and I am finishing it." (She also has an Internal pattern.) This was the third attempt, and she managed to build in many different projects towards her Masters degree. For her thesis, she conducted a research project in Asia to complete her degree, while her husband was

"Hamster migration—
every seven years."

there on sabbatical. She found a way to *build her need for Difference into her activities.*

Her husband has a Sameness with Exception pattern for several Contexts. He is motivated by evolution and progression, while she prefers to have things changing all the time. How can this work in a marriage? Since none of us is actually living in Reality, who cares what your spouse's patterns may be as long as he *thinks it is getting better* and *she thinks it is totally different*? And so long as he does not bang his shins on the furniture when she moves it around.

For couples with different patterns, I would suggest that you understand your own need for change, as well as your spouse's, and make sure you each feel your needs are being met.

Revolutions and Evolutions: Hiring

There are several things to think about when doing a Job Profile in preparation for hiring. Does the job require a great variety of tasks? How long does each task remain the same? Does the successful fulfillment of the objectives demand creating a revolution (Difference), building upon what is already there (Sameness with Exception), or maintaining the status quo (Sameness)? How much of each?

You can predict that people with a high Difference pattern will create revolutions around them, especially if they also have Proactive and Options patterns. In fact, someone with a combination of Options and Difference can be a compulsive change-artist. I wanted to call on a client with this pattern after not seeing him for two years. I tried the company where he had been working. He had, of course, left and gone somewhere else.

I profiled a man, and told him about his Difference pattern and what that meant for his career. He retorted that he had been a high school teacher and principal for thirty years. I asked him in how many schools had he worked. He had been in *seventeen different schools.* Knowing this pattern will allow you to predict someone's past—a great party trick.

Since the majority of people (65%) in the work Context have a Sameness with Exception pattern, you will be more likely to find those candidates. Many jobs need someone who can build and progress. A fewer number of positions actually require revolutionaries.

People Management

Employees with a Sameness pattern do not respond well to change. They are well suited to tasks that do not change, such as many administrative or production tasks. Managers with this pattern strive to keep standards up and want to provide continuity. This attribute is also appropriate for maintaining a long-term rapport with clients. To motivate Sameness employees, talk about what this task has in common with what they already know.

Sameness with Exception employees will accept change once a year as long as it is not too drastic. They will feel stressed if placed in high-change environments, which explains the stress-related illnesses rampant in the post-recessionary nineties. They are motivated when they can perceive a *progression* in their work. To get them interested in a task, you can tell them how it will make things better, or will build on what they are already doing.

I've Been Moved

To capture the interest of someone with a Difference pattern, you will need to give them lots of different things to work on. Get them to change things (if they are also Proactive) or create changes for them to respond to (if they are Reactive). For some companies this happens frequently anyway. A group of IBM European headquarters managers told me the nickname they have for IBM is "I've Been Moved." Europeans are not used to the American habit of moving people around every few years. (I also heard that the nickname given to the European headquarters of IBM was "La cage aux foils" because no one makes a presentation without overhead foils.*)

Difference people will need to hear how what they are doing is totally different. Remember the line from Monty Python's Flying Circus? "And now for something completely different."

Taking the Pain out of Organizational Change

Once upon a time, large companies had work groups that were called typing pools. Many of the people who worked in typing pools stayed there for a long time, sometimes fifteen, twenty or twenty-five years, typing documents all day long. Then a miracle occurred. Word processors were invented. The agents of change were very excited by all the *different possibilities* these wonderful new machines could offer. They heralded the arrival of the miraculous machines by announcing to the people working in the typing pools: "We have bought some *totally new machines* which are going to *revolutionize* how you do your work." Many people resigned. Countless more panicked and said "I'm too old to learn this. I can't do this. I am a failure." Now, typing pools have completely disappeared from the workplace.

The moral of the story has little to do with the revolutionary machines. If you had been typing for over fifteen years, would you really be interested in revolution? The **language** of change created much unnecessary resistance in the workforce. Forget the word *new*. Forget the word *revolution*. A more appropriate language for populations with Sameness and Procedures patterns would be: "We have bought some machines which are *exactly like* a typewriter. They have the *same* keyboard. They have a *few* extra keys which allow you to go *faster*, work *better*, correct mistakes *easier*,

---

*"Foils" is the British term for overhead transparencies.

but *essentially, they're the same*. And we'll *teach you the procedure* for using them."

From the mid-1980s to the early 1990s, organizations began to notice that large numbers of their workforce balked at frequent changes. Many introduced "Continuous Improvement" programs. They were not called "Dramatic Difference" programs.

The introduction of workstations, personal and networked computers, and statistical process control on the shop floor was (and is) often mishandled in the same way. It is important to prepare the groundwork for major technological and organizational changes. Knowing your workforce and planning your announcements and implementation, by matching the language you use with the people affected, can *dramatically improve* the chances of making the change stick. Resistance is not a necessary outcome of change programs.

I have noticed that those responsible for introducing or implementing change in organizations frequently have a high personal need for change. Often they are mismatched with their environment, and so, *do not speak the same language* as the people they wish to influence.

Why New Coke Didn't Make It

Once again, there is no substitute for good market research. Remember New Coke? Apparently, when they tested the taste of New Coke, the results were conclusive: New Coke tasted better than the old Coke. However, they could not have tested the *name*.

Let's examine, for a moment, the distribution of the patterns in this category. Only a maximum of 30 percent of the population in the work Context is interested in *new*, according to Rodger Bailey's work. But this was the soft drink Context. How many people do you think would want to drink something new in soft drinks, as opposed to what they know, trust, and buy consistently? Apparently, not very many. Coca Cola responded and returned old Coke to the market. They called it Coke Classic, which is Sameness language.

Labatt Blue, a Canadian beer, apparently understood the pattern. They produced a billboard campaign with the slogan: "Tired of the same, old thing? Neither are we."

In 1992 the Saturn automobile was introduced. The commercials announced: "A different kind of company. A different kind of car." My ears perked up immediately. It would be interesting to find out what percentage of the new-car market actually wants something completely different.

When your market has mainly a Sameness pattern, you will need to demonstrate how the product will give them something they know. It must look, sound, and feel like old *reliable*. "You can always count on us" or "We'll always be there," like Roch Voisine's hit song. This can be a creative challenge for new products and services. How about: "Remember when you . . . ? It's back, just the same, and better than ever before."

Sameness with Exception customers want improvements. Show them how your product or service is better than the competition or what they had before, how it will make their lives easier (Toward), with fewer hassles (Away From). They will prefer to buy *upgrades* rather than different software packages.

Difference people want something totally new and different from everyone else: "You'll be the only one in your neighbourhood" (External) or "You can see for yourself how unique this is" (Internal).

If you want to capture everyone, you will need an updated version of *new* and *improved*, since that slogan is now old hat.

Purchasers and Users of Software

Software purchasing and using presents an interesting Context. From my work with some major software companies, my clients and I happened on an interesting conflict of patterns. With regards to the corporate purchasers of software, we have noticed that they seem to have an Options and Difference combination. They want upgrades and new software to look and be totally different, with many more possible applications, even if they do not need them right away. Contrast this with the poor end-user, who suffers through each new installation, having to learn everything all over again. End-users tend to have a Sameness and Procedures combination. (So do I when it comes to software—at this writing, I still haven't upgraded to Windows 95 because I'm afraid I'll have to spend hours and hours learning how to use it.)

For my software clients, we have developed marketing materials and sales processes to reflect both the patterns of the purchasers and the end-users. Part of the process includes educating the purchasers on how to get more enthusiasm from the end-users, and less resistance to new upgrades.

Summary

≋

Decision Factors

Question: What is the relationship between (your work this year and last year)?

Sameness:	They like things to stay the same. They will provoke change only every 15 to 25 years.
Sameness with Exception:	They prefer situations to evolve over time. They want major change about every 5 to 7 years.
Difference:	They want change to be constant and drastic. They will initiate change every 1 to 2 years.
Sameness with Exception and Difference:	They like both evolution and revolution. Major change averages every 3 to 4 years.
Distribution:	Sameness 5% Sameness with Exception 65% Difference 20% Sameness with Exception and Difference 10%

Influencing Language

Sameness:	the same as; as you already know; like before; identical
Sameness with Exception:	more; better; less; the same except; evolving; progress; gradual improvement; upgrade
Difference:	new; totally different; completely changes; switch; shift; unique; one of a kind; brand new
Sameness with Exception and Difference:	Use *both* Sameness with Exception *and* Difference language

Using the Profiling Worksheet: Motivation Traits

≋

On the following page you will find the Motivation Traits worksheet to help you master both asking the LAB Profile questions and recognizing the patterns of the person you are interviewing. A similar worksheet can be found at the end of the Working Traits section. The full profiling sheet (for both the Motivation and Working Traits) is included near the end of the book.

On the left side of the page are the questions to ask. I have emphasized in **bold** the basic questions, while the Context is in *script*. Remember that for LEVEL (Proactive and Reactive), there are no questions to ask. You simply listen for the patterns while the person is talking.

On the right side of the chart are the patterns and a summary of each of the clues for recognizing the patterns.

When I am interviewing someone I usually start off by putting one check mark each on Proactive and Reactive, since 60 to 65 percent of the population is right in the middle. Subsequently during the interview, if they use mostly one pattern or the other, I add check marks in the appropriate place.

Often I will write down the expressions that indicate a particular pattern, so that I can verify them when I review the results with the person.

Giving Feedback

When sharing the results of the LAB Profile with someone, avoid using jargon such as *Toward* or *Away From*. It will be more meaningful if you simply describe the behaviours of each pattern. For example: "You prefer to solve problems and do troubleshooting rather than working toward goals. What triggers you into action is when there is a problem to be solved or prevented."

I have included a pattern summary in the Appendix to help you use layperson's terminology when speaking to the uninitiated.

The LAB Worksheet: Motivation Traits

Name: _____	Company: _____
Profiler: _____	Position: _____
Date: _____	Context: _____

Questions	Categories	Patterns—Indicators
(no question for Level)	**LEVEL**	_____ **Proactive**—*action, do it, short, crisp sentences* _____ **Reactive**—*try, think about it, could, wait*
• **What do you want in your (work)?**	**CRITERIA**	
• **Why is that (criteria) important?** (ask up to 3 times)	**DIRECTION**	_____ **Toward**—*attain, gain, achieve, get, include* _____ **Away From**—*avoid, exclude, recognize problems*
• **How do you know you have done a good job (at . . .) ?**	**SOURCE**	_____ **Internal**—*knows within self* _____ **External**—*told by others, facts and figures*
• **Why did you choose (your current work)?**	**REASON**	_____ **Options**—*criteria, choice, possibilities, variety* _____ **Procedures**—*story, how, necessity, didn't choose*
• **What is the relationship between (your work this year and last year)?**	**DECISION FACTORS**	_____ **Sameness**—*same, no change* _____ **Sameness with Exception**—*more, better, comparisons* _____ **Difference**—*change, new, unique* _____ **Sameness with Exception & Difference**—*new and comparisons*

Part 3

Working Traits

Working Traits

Questions	Categories	Patterns—Indicators
(no questions for **Scope and Attention Direction**)	**SCOPE** _____ **Specific**—*details, sequences, exactly* _____ **General**—*Overview, big picture, random order*	
	ATTENTION DIRECTION _____ **Self**—*short monotone responses* _____ **Other**—*animated, expressive, automatic responses*	
• Tell me about a (*work situation*) that gave you trouble.	**STRESS RESPONSE** _____ **Feeling**—*goes in and stays in feelings* _____ **Choice**—*goes in and out of feelings* _____ **Thinking**—*doesn't go into feelings*	
• Tell me about a (*work situation*) that was (*criteria*). (wait for answer) • What did you like about it?	**STYLE** _____ **Independent**—*alone, I, sole responsibility* _____ **Proximity**—*in control, others around* _____ **Co-operative**—*we, team, share responsibility*	
	ORGANIZATION _____ **Person**—*people, feelings, reactions* _____ **Thing**—*tools, tasks, ideas*	
• What is a good way for you to increase your success at (*your work*)? • What is a good way for someone else to increase their success at (*their work*)?	**RULE STRUCTURE** _____ **My/My**—*My rules for me/My rules for you* _____ **My/. (period)**—*My rules for me/ Who cares?* _____ **No/My**—*No rules for me/My rules for you* _____ **My/Your**—*My rules for me/Your rules for you*	
• How do you know that someone else (*an equal of yours*) is good at their (*work*)? • How many times do you have to (*see, hear, read, do*) that to be convinced they are good?	**CONVINCER** _____ **See** _____ **Hear** _____ **Read** _____ **Do**	**# of Examples**—*give number* **Automatic**—*benefit of the doubt* **Consistent**—*not completely convinced* **Period of Time**—*give time period*

Working Traits

≋

The next eight categories of the LAB Profile will tell you how people deal with information, what type of tasks and environment they need to be most productive in a given Context, and how they get convinced about something.

These categories will demonstrate how to *maintain* someone's motivation. Each pattern is described in its pure form.

At the end of the Working Traits section, you will find another Summary Profiling Worksheet to help you master asking the Working Traits questions and recognizing the patterns.

The Forest for the Trees: Working Scope

> *What size chunk of information does the person handle*
> *best? The big picture or specific details?*

Using the Scope category, you can determine whether someone can handle overviews and grand designs, or whether the details make more sense. There are two patterns in this category:

Specific

Specific people handle small pieces of information well. At the extreme, they cannot perceive or create an overview. They treat information in linear *sequences*, step by step, in all its detail. A Specific person perceives the trees, branches, and twigs, rather than the forest. They may have difficulty prioritizing as a result. If they are interrupted in the middle of a sequence, they tend to either start over at the beginning or resume the telling from the point at which they were interrupted. Specific people work well where details must be attended to, in tasks such as organizing events or handling logistics.

Note: There is a difference between a *sequence*, which Specific people use and a *procedure*, used by Procedures people. While both have a beginning and an end, there may be choice points, branches and several end points in a procedure. A sequence is chronological, linear, narrow and unidirectional. It is possible for a person to *have both* Specific and Options patterns or a Procedures pattern in combination with a General pattern.

Sequence: A — B — C — D etc.

```
                        | --------- C ------- > -------- G ------- H
Procedure:    A ------- B        | -------- E
                        | --------- D
                                 | -------- F
```

General

People with a General pattern in a given Context prefer to work on the *overview*, or at the *conceptual level*, though they can concentrate on details for finite periods of time. Because they see the *big picture* all at once, they may present ideas in a random order without stating the link between one thought and another. They concentrate on the forest; having to deal with the trees for long periods of time irritates them.

Distribution _____ %

(in the work Context, from Rodger Bailey)

Specific	Equally Specific & General	General
15%	25%	60%

Pattern Recognition
≋

While there are no specific questions for this category, you will be able to recognize the patterns within virtually each sentence spoken.

Hint: One simple way you can know for sure is to time your LAB Profile interview. On average, a full interview takes about 20 minutes to complete, not including giving the person your feedback. With a Specific person, the interview will be at least 40 minutes.

Here's how to recognize these patterns in conversation:

Specific
- speak in sequences, step-by-step
- *lots* of modifiers, adverbs, adjectives
- proper nouns for people, places, and things
- if they lose the sequence, they will start over again or continue from where they left off
- only seem to be aware of the step before and after the one they are on; not much perception of the overview

General
- may present things in random order
- overview, summaries
- concepts, abstracts
- simple sentences, few modifiers or details

Examples

Specific:	"Yesterday at 10 A.M. George and I met with Mr. Vivaldi, our big client from Rome, who spoke about renewing our shipping contract for the third year in a row. He now wants the price of the cardboard packaging to be included with the total price next year."
Mainly Specific:	"Yesterday at 10 A.M. George and I met with Mr.Vivaldi, our client from Rome, to discuss renewing our shipping contract. He wants to include the packaging in the total deal."
Equally Specific and General:	"Yesterday, Mr. Vivaldi told George and me that he wants to include the cardboard packaging in the price next year."
Mainly General:	"Next year Mr. Vivaldi wants to renegotiate our contract."
General:	"Rome wants to renegotiate."

Combinations

I am often asked, when someone is answering the Reason question from the Motivation Traits, how one would know if they were Specific or Procedures, if they are telling a story. The Reason question is: "Why did you choose your current work?" To distinguish between a Procedure pattern and a sequence, which is Specific, you will need to pay attention to the amount of detail given.

Here are some examples. The first one is a response from a Procedures person who has a mainly General pattern. "I didn't really choose this kind of work. I was working in another company and they laid off a lot of people. I didn't have a job when this one came up. I applied and got it." Procedures, mainly General.

Here is an example of Procedures with Mainly Specific. "I was working for the Whoofed Cookies Beverage Company as a field engineer from 1973 to 1991. Then the company went into a period of financial difficulties, so in order to stop themselves from going under, they had to let 250 people go. They closed down my department and then I spent eight and a half months unemployed. I had made thirty applications in each of three geographical areas. Then Stephanie Slobdonovich from the Miracle Cure Cleaning Company called me; I had an interview the following day at 10 A.M. and was hired."

Here is what Specific and Options would sound like. "It was exactly the kind of thing I was looking for. I get to work with people. Different kinds of people. I get to work with tall people, short people, fat people, thin people. People with curly hair and people with thin hair and people with no hair on the top of their heads . . . etc." This is not a story; it is all Criteria (therefore Options), and described in what I would call, excruciating detail. (If I have characterized that example as *excruciating*, what does that tell you about my own pattern?)

Here's another general hint:

As you become increasingly familiar with recognizing the patterns in everyday conversation, you will find yourself noticing and hearing many patterns at once, sometimes within a single sentence.

Influencing Language

Generally speaking, it is important to match a person's pattern in exactly the way they talk to you when in conversation.

Specific
- exactly; precisely; specifically; details; use sequences and lots of qualifiers

General
- the big picture; the main idea; essentially; the important thing is; in general; concepts
- leave out the details and multiple qualifiers

When Bad Communication Happens to Good People

When a person with a General pattern is communicating, negotiating, or problem-solving with a Specific person, you may notice many misunderstandings. The Specific person may be concentrating on each separate example of a problem, for example, and listing what happened in chronological order, while the General person wants to get to the point. There is a huge difference in the size of pieces of information each is treating; one is dealing with each item in great detail, while the other is trying to get at the big picture. Several things will happen:

1. While the General person will be able to follow the specifics for awhile, he will quickly get bored or feel drowned in detail and want to quit, leave or yell, depending on his preferences.
2. The Specific person will insist on giving ever more details of information in an attempt to make things precise for the other person, and will not understand the attempts of the General person to summarize the situation.
3. The General person may speak in such vague terms that she does not give enough information for others to understand what she is actually talking about. She may then lose credibility with the Specific person, who may suspect her of bad intentions.

So what is the cure? There are several options. (Wouldn't you know it?) First, you will need to realize that this situation will take some time to resolve, because of one party's need for detail. This can be an advantage where the specifics of a contractual agreement need to be sorted out properly, and will save time later, as they will not be overlooked. (You would have to have somewhat of a General and a Toward pattern to *overlook* something.)

You could ask a person who has both Specific and General to mediate between the two, essentially *translating* back and forth. If you are mediating, you will need to reassure both parties that their respective approaches are important and relevant, however different they may be.

For the Specific person, you will need to play back their issues and Criteria, and then describe the sequence by which you will proceed, which includes translating items into General terms. For the General person, give them the big picture. "The main thing is making sure you both can understand each other; I'll help by facilitating that process."

Other alternatives include getting the Specific person to make a list of the important issues on one page in order to facilitate the General person's understanding. To help a General person be more clear to a Specific person, ask them sensory-specific questions such as "How would you know when it's right?" or "Can you give me a tangible example?" or "What specifically would have to happen?"

To capitalize on the strengths of each one, have the Specific person check the details of any agreement (especially if they are also Away From, so they can pick out errors and omissions). The General person will be able to determine whether the process is generally on track to achieving an agreement.

The key is making sure that each understand how they themselves and the other person are functioning. They can use these complementary differences to mutual benefit, provided they accept them and adjust the process, as mentioned above, to take into account each person's needs and strengths.

When someone is highly Specific, how can you interact with them to help speed them through to the end of their sequence? One of the things you can do is ask them what happens at the end. This may be perceived as a sort of violation, but at least it is not an interruption.

Why Do All the Songs I Know End in La, La, La?

Here is an analogy to illustrate how someone with a Specific pattern processes information. When people want to remember the words to a song, they usually start singing the song from the beginning, because the words are stored in their brain sequentially. If you interrupt them, they lose their train of thought, and will have to go back to the beginning to pick it up again. Simply talking and responding will not make them go back; it is *being interrupted* that makes them start over. Asking them "then what happened?" may help them to get to the next item. By doing that, you are respecting the sequence and moving them on to the next step. The word "then" presupposes that something happened before, and something happened after. Another suggestion, if they do not have an off-the-scale Specific pattern, is to ask them to fast-forward, almost as if they had recorded their thoughts on tape.

Hiring

Does the job require close attention to specific, sequential details for extended periods of time, or is detailed work of this kind only a small part of the overall responsibilities? Bookkeeping requires someone who can concentrate on specifics for long stretches at a time; deciding financial strategies is much more an overview kind of task. People and project management tend to be Mainly General functions.

Many positions in manufacturing are Specific and sequential in nature, such as assembly-line work. General people would make many mistakes through inattention to detail in this kind of work. Quality control necessitates a Mainly Specific pattern as well as Procedures and Away From.

The essential question to answer when profiling a position is to *what extent is attention to detail necessary*? You would not want a pharmacist to generally get the dosage right when dispensing a prescription.

Difficult Bosses

If a manager has equal preference for Specific and General, she can be very difficult to work for. This kind of manager not only knows *what* needs to be done, but tends to become very specific in telling employees exactly *how* to do it. Because they, as managers, have a handle on both aspects of the work, they often do not delegate, believing that it is easier to just do it themselves, or that they can do a better job themselves. When combined with a Co-operative pattern (please refer to Working Style), they do not leave any territory for their employees to deal with on their own.

One of the advantages of having an equal aptitude for the detail and the big picture is that this person can handle complex tasks and analyses. She can attend to any level or the whole thing.

Sales, Marketing, and Submitting Bids

Prospective purchasers who have a General pattern will want broad descriptions that match their Criteria. As can be expected, Specific people want all the facts, listed in order. Print advertisements for technical products or software often contain a lot of specifics right in the ad. These ads could be accompanied by another one for General purchasers, with a compelling image and a few words.

Many companies, when submitting a bid, do not know whether the purchasing group consists of mainly Specific or General people or both. Why take a chance on either giving too much information or not enough?

Bids *must* contain a lot of detail. The *Executive Overview* will be read by the Generals, with an occasional peek in the Index to find the specific bits they need to complete the picture. The Specifics and people with a mixed pattern will need the full text to make their decision.

Life, the Universe, and Everything

In Douglas Adams' famous science fiction novel, *The Hitchhikers Guide to the Galaxy*, the great question of life, the universe, and everything was asked of the biggest computer ever built. After centuries of computation, and much speculation on the part of Galaxy philosophers, the wonderful computer submitted its answer to the waiting populations. The answer was: 42. Well, what can you expect when you address a General question to a Specific entity?

Pies in the Sky

One of the problems encountered by people who are "pie in the sky" General has to do with the consequences of staying in the conceptual realm. A friend of mine who has a General and Reactive combination had been the head of Human Resources for a large firm in France. He and the company went their separate ways because of some political disagreements.

I asked him, "What are you going to do next?" He responded, "It is important, when one is to work with a company, that the policies and values be the same and what is really important to me is that we establish a humanistic philosophy." I said: "Okay. What are you going to do next to find that kind of company?" He continued: "It is important to understand that the philosophy must be right." I began to lose it: " So what are you going to **do** to find a job?" I shrieked. He needed to break the task of making his next career move into smaller steps and to have a plan of action for meeting his Criteria.

People who are very General may present things in random order (how's that for an oxymoron?), because they are looking at the big picture. They sometimes do not bother specifying the link between items or ideas, since they can see the whole relationship. Often people will not know what they are talking about.

We have discussed the two patterns. Do you get the picture? Or do I need to go into more detail?

Summary

≋

Scope

Question: There is no question for this category.

Specific:	Deals with details and sequences. Cannot see the overview.
General:	Prefers the overview, big picture. Can handle details for short periods.
Distribution:	Specific 15%
	Equally Specific and General 25%
	General 60%
	(from Rodger Bailey, in the Context of work)

Influencing Language

Specific:	exactly; precisely; specifically; gives lots of details
General:	the big picture; essentially; the point is; in general

When Hinting Won't Work: Working Attention Direction

> *Does the person naturally pay attention to the nonverbal behaviour of others, or to their own internal experience?*

The Attention Direction category reveals whether a person can perceive, and respond *automatically* to, the body language and voice tone of other people or not. There are two patterns:

Self

Self people do not show many emotions, although they do have feelings. There is sometimes a time gap between when they receive a stimulus and when they respond to it. They respond based on what *they* consider to be appropriate. These people are convinced only by the *content* of what people say, rather than the accompanying tone, body language, or level of rapport. They have difficulty establishing rapport because they do not notice other people's body language, and therefore they miss many clues. People with this pattern simply do not pick up hints.

They know how well the communication is going, based only on their own feelings. As a result, they tend not to be adept at interpersonal communication. At work, many Self people become technical experts in fields where communication skills are not essential.

Other

Other people have automatic reflex reactions to people's behaviours. They are animated (for their culture) and respond to others with facial expressions, body movements, and shifts in voice tone. They know how the communication is going based on the *responses* they *consciously or unconsciously* observe from the other person. These people are good at creating and maintaining rapport, provided they also have the other appropriate patterns.

Distribution _____ **%**

(in the work Context, from Rodger Bailey)

Self	**Other**
7%	93%

One in Fourteen People

According to Rodger Bailey's research in the work Context, approximately one in every fourteen people you will meet will have a mainly Self pattern, if these statistics also hold true for the general population. From my experience, I believe that you will find more who are somewhere in the middle between the two patterns.

Pattern Recognition
≋

There is no verbal test for this pattern, as it shows up in body language or the absence thereof. To test for Attention Direction, I usually drop a pencil accidentally on purpose. People with an Other pattern will spontaneously bend down and pick it up, provided they have seen it or heard it drop. Self people will not pick it up. When speaking to someone on the phone, I will sneeze or have a coughing fit in the middle of a sentence. Does the person say their cultural equivalent of Gesundheit or continue on as if nothing had happened?

The following clues will also be apparent throughout the conversation:

Self
- Absence of culturally appropriate behavioural responses such as head nodding, saying "uh-huh," etc.
- reacts only to the content of what you say
- doesn't "pick up the pencil"
- doesn't notice or respond to your voice tone
- little or no facial expression or voice variation

Other
- responds to both content and nonverbal aspects of the communication
- will nod head, move body, say "uh-huh", etc., as a response
- animated (for their culture)

Let's say I were speaking to someone who had a Self pattern and I, with my shoulders drooped, my bottom lip sticking out, and a whiny tone of voice, said: "I'm really happy to be here." She or he would think that I *was* really happy to be here. For this kind of person, unless you actually say: "I am annoyed and irritated" explicitly, they do not pick it up. Hinting will not work, nor will sarcasm as a method of communication.

While only 7 percent of the population at work are Self; probably many more are borderline; that is, they have some of the Self pattern. You can recognize those people when you drop the pencil. They look at the pencil, they look at you, they look at the pencil, and then they may eventually decide to pick it up. It is not spontaneous, not a reflex. A reflex action is something outside of voluntary control. Sometimes you can also recognize these borderline people because, although they may exhibit little nonverbal behaviour themselves (i.e., facial expressions, gestures, and voice variation), they may be able to notice and respond to the nonverbal behaviour of others.

Examples

There are no word examples for this category. Only behaviour observation will allow you to identify "Self" and "Other" patterns.

Here is an example from American television. In a program called M*A*S*H, a character named Radar always knew what the other characters wanted or were feeling before they did. He was picking up signals and clues in a highly intuitive manner, an off-the-scale Other.

For a Self example, we can recall Pat Paulsen, a deadpan comedian who ran for President of the United States more than once in the 1960s. He spoke in a completely toneless manner with a total absence of facial expression or gestures.

When I was leading one of a series of communication and conflict resolution seminars at the CERN (European Centre for Nuclear Research) in Geneva, there was an engineer who had a strong Self pattern. Much to the annoyance of other participants, he kept stopping the discussion to ask for more explicit definitions of terms. He was filtering for the *content* of what was being said. I asked the participants to do an exercise in groups where they were going to practise some confrontation techniques. One person was supposed to observe and give feedback while they each took turns role-playing. When I went into his group, he was practically in tears because, although he had understood that there was something to be observed, he just could not see or hear anything. I had to do some on-the-spot counselling to help him focus on what *was* possible for him to do.

The definition of a good host or hostess is knowing what your guests want before they become aware of it themselves. For example, when you are in someone's home and cannot find your salad fork, without your having to ask, does one of your hosts notice your dilemma and go get you one? A Self person would not have noticed that you needed one. You would have had to ask for it.

Communication

Some people have asked me if a Self person would feel uncomfortable in social situations. How does a person with a Self pattern usually know if the communication is going well? They will focus on what is being said, and how they themselves feel about it, without noticing the nuances of nonverbal communication, and so may feel quite comfortable. An Other person can evaluate the communication by unconsciously picking up body-language cues and listening to tone of voice. What is more likely is that the Other people, in communication with a Self person, might feel more uncomfortable because of the absence of the nonverbal responses by which they normally get feedback.

When communicating with an Other person, the quality of the rapport that you established is just as important to them as the substance of what you are communicating. Self people are not influenced by the level of rapport you have with them, so you will need to be absolutely rigorous in the presentation of your arguments or explanations.

Hiring

Self people usually do not succeed in work that requires the ability to create and maintain rapport. They are not suited for customer-service work or dealing with angry customers. Self people do well where technical expertise is required.

In the 1980s while I was conducting a series of interpersonal communications courses in a large high tech company, I could often tell a participant was from the Information Services department, usually within the first five minutes of conversation. Many Self people became technical experts in information technology and other technical knowledge-based fields. They tend to do well there, except in situations where knowing how to play office politics is an asset.

Having made that generalization, I must say that I have since noticed many more Other people working in information services than a few years ago, as companies increasingly demand both technical and interpersonal skills. As many of you know first-hand, electronic mail aficionados have even worked out ways to express feelings in text, by including voice tone and emotions in "emoticons" such as :-) (grin), ;-) (wink), :-((sad), :-Q (close but no cigar), and so on. Using the UPPER CASE indicates SHOUTING. (My personal favourite is: *%-), which indicates that *I am having a bad hair day and I don't care.*)

Other people, provided they also have the Choice pattern from the Stress Response category, have the ability to empathize with others.

Once a Self, Always a Self?

In theory, the Self pattern can be either *uni-contextual* or *transcontextual*. Transcontextual means that the pattern exists across many Contexts for a person. Both are possible. In my experience to date, I have noticed more Self people who have this pattern across several Contexts than those who are Self in only one Context and not in another. One student told me about her husband, who "never seemed to notice what was going on." She felt she always had to *tell* him.

My advice would be that it is more rigorous to test in different Contexts, rather than just assuming that someone who has a Self pattern will always have that pattern.

Influencing Language

Pay attention to both the level of rapport you have established and make sure that your propositions hold water logically. Remember Mr. Spock?

Self
- keep the communication focused on the content
- match their Criteria and Convincer Channel and Mode

Other
- they are influenced by the depth of rapport

There is no specific Influencing Language for Self people. Pay attention to your content because the relationship is not what they filter for. Be totally rigorous in what you say. Define your terms properly. If they also have an Away From pattern, they will cut your argument to pieces, if it does not completely hold water. There is no point in taking it personally; that is just how they function.

Summary
≋

Attention Direction

Question: There is no question for this category.

Self:	Attends to own experience. Doesn't notice nonverbal behaviour or voice tone.
Other:	Has automatic reflex responses to nonverbal behaviour.
Distribution:	Self 7% Other 93%

Influencing Language

Self:	Focus on the content, match their Criteria and Convincer Channel and Mode.
Other:	They are influenced by the depth of rapport.

$\mathcal{F}$reaked Out or Cool as a Cucumber: Working Stress Response

≋

How does a person react to stress in the work Context?

Wouldn't you like to have a way to find out in *five minutes or less*, if someone can handle a high-stress job?

The Stress Response category examines how you respond to the pressures, at work or elsewhere, that are *typical* for the Context you are in. This is not about how someone would respond to major life dramas, since almost everyone would have an emotional response in those situations. People respond to these "normal" pressures in the following three ways:

Feeling

People with a Feeling pattern have emotional responses to the *normal* levels of stress at work. They go into their emotions and *stay there*. High-stress jobs can therefore be difficult for them to handle over the long term. To many other people, they seem to overreact to situations or be hypersensitive. They are well suited for artistic or creative work, where emotion provides the juice. As salespeople, they find it difficult to handle rejection and may not, as a result, prospect for new customers as often as they should.

Choice

Choice people first have an emotional response to the normal stresses at work and then either return to an unemotional state or not as they desire, in a given situation. *They have choice.* Because they feel emotions themselves, they can empathize with others, or choose not to. They tend to perform well as people-managers, as they can combine the personal side of the job and distance themselves when necessary.

Thinking

People with a Thinking pattern do not have emotional responses to the *normal* stressful situations for a given Context. They have trouble empathizing with others, as they themselves do not go into emotional states. They will not panic in most emergencies, but keep a cool head. They are reliable performers in high-stress jobs.

Distribution _____ **%**

(in the work Context, from Rodger Bailey)		
Feeling	**Choice**	**Thinking**
15%	70%	15%

Pattern Recognition
≋

Question: TELL ME ABOUT A WORK SITUATION THAT CAUSED YOU TROUBLE.

For Contexts other than work, simply substitute the Context for "work situation." That is, tell me about a buying decision that caused you trouble.

When you are asking this question, avoid having the person tell you about *all* the times they had a particular kind of problem. "Whenever a customer is unhappy with our service, I get nervous." Make sure the person picks one specific troublesome (not catastrophic) situation that he remembers. What you are to determine, as they review that situation, is if they go into an emotional state and get stuck there, have an emotional response and come out of it, or have no emotional reaction at all.

Nonverbal Indicators

For the Stress Response category, there are no specific language patterns to listen for. To recognize the pattern, you will need to observe and listen for nonverbal cues, changes in how the person behaves.

Feeling
- they visibly and vocally have an emotional response while describing a difficult situation
- changes in 3 or more of the following are indicators of a change in emotional state:
  body posture, gestures
  facial muscle tension
  eyes drop
  voice will change in timbre, tone, speed and volume

- will stay in their emotional state throughout their recital

Choice
- will go into their emotions initially and return at least once

Thinking
- will not go into their emotions

Warning: It is possible, when you ask this question, that the other person (if they have a Feeling pattern or if they choose to talk about a major catastrophe) may go into a highly negative or painful emotional state. For this reason, make sure that you ask the Stress Response question before the Style and Organization questions: "Tell me about a working experience that was (*your positive Criteria*). What did you like about it?" It is important to ensure that you do not leave someone in a negative state. Reminding them of situations associated with their positive Criteria will help shift them into a more positive frame of mind. If they seem to still be distressed, you may also have them change seats to help them get out of the negative state.

Examples

These patterns can only be recognized by observing and listening to those behaviour changes listed above, not in the language structure.

For a demonstration of the three patterns, please refer to my audio-cassette series *Understanding and Triggering Motivation: The LAB Profile.*[1]

For a good example of the Choice pattern, watch Captain Kathryn Janeway (played by Kate Mulgrew) on the *Star Trek: Voyager* television series.

Hiring

It is very useful to pay attention to this pattern, because certain professions demand certain kinds of responses. For example, the Thinking pattern would be most appropriate for an airline pilot or an air traffic controller. Could you imagine what would happen if a high Feeling airline pilot were to notice another airplane aiming right for her plane? Air traffic controllers whom I trained told me that you usually can tell if the person beside you is having a *close incident*. The heat energy apparently *just pours out*.

If rapport and empathy are important in a job, then Choice is the best pattern to have. Choice people have feelings and can also come out of an emotional state, if appropriate, to look at the situation or take action. When you regularly experience emotions yourself, you can more easily recognize that other people also have feelings. If Harry stays on the analytical, thinking level as a response to Sally's feelings, he probably will not acknowledge the importance of Sally's feelings to her, or even sympathize with them.

---

1. See the Resources section for details

Many people in artistic careers have the Feeling pattern, because art is often an expression of feelings and emotions. I discovered that the principal activity of the staff in many fine dining establishments (especially in Europe) is not customer service, but trying to keep the chef happy. Many chefs are highly emotional people. When they go over the edge about something, all hell breaks loose.

Incompetency Attacks

In sales positions, Feeling people often become demoralized when faced with rejection from prospective customers, because they take it personally. It means that they would often feel stressed in that kind of function, and may even be prone to what a friend of mine calls *Incompetency Attacks*. An Incompetency Attack has nothing to do with one's real level of competence, which may be excellent. It is a strong, emotionally based belief of incompetence, usually felt by someone with a Feeling pattern in that Context.

Career Counselling

When I am counselling someone about career choices, I pay close attention to this pattern, because it gives an indication of how much stress the person can handle.

Passion

There are some other issues to consider. While a high Feeling person may be prone to suffering from stress, they also have a *need* for passion and intensity. When a person has both Feeling and Options patterns in a Context, they are highly passionate about developing alternatives, a very creative combination.

Managing Stress and People

According to Rodger Bailey, most of the population at work has the Choice pattern (70%). This means that when faced with a difficult or troublesome situation they will first have an emotional response. As a manager you can assist by helping these people *disassociate* themselves from their feelings, if appropriate, by helping them change perspectives.

There are a couple of ways to do this. You can distort time by asking them: "Can you imagine what we'll think about this situation two years from now?" You can have them see it from someone else's viewpoint: "I don't think our customers will care much about this." Or you can have them view the whole thing from the outside: "If you were a fly on the wall when this happened, what would you notice?"

For Feeling people you will probably have to practise your conflict resolution and mediation skills. To maintain their motivation, give them tasks that they can get passionate about. As they are working, watch for signs of distress and overload of tension. These people are the most likely to suffer from stress-related illnesses because they feel stressed more often than people with the other patterns. Feeling people may overreact, particularly in tense or conflictual circumstances. It would be useful for them to learn how to dissociate or cool off. (See B'Elanna Torres played by Roxann Biggs-Dawson, the half-human, half-Klingon in *Star Trek: Voyager*, for a clear example of a Feeling pattern.)

When faced with a highly intense reaction from an employee, create rapport by raising your tone to the same level as his while saying something positive or surprising: "I'm so upset about you being upset, that I am ready to tear my hair out!" Saying something like that will get their attention, so that you can then channel their energy onto a more productive path.

Thinking people are highly appreciated where there is need for someone with a cool head. These people spend much time already disassociated from their feelings and can be called on when a rational approach is needed. Do not expect them, however, to create rapport with others who are in an emotional state, because they will have no sympathy. Thinking people, particularly if they have a combination with Internal, can, however, take the heat and be able to stay in the kitchen!

Influencing Language

You can *rouse* people in an extraordinary way by simply *being there* and making *rational sense* of it all.

Feeling
- get them excited about something and focus on the emotion, using words such as:
    intense; exciting; mind boggling; extraordinary, etc.

Choice
- speak in terms that indicate you can go in and out of an emotional state:
    i.e., "You can get excited about this, and then realize that it makes good sense too."

Thinking
- present the *logical* facts:
    the cold reality; hard facts; clear thinking; statistics

Language Range and Culture

The use of highly emotional words is not necessarily an indicator of a Feeling pattern. Some cultures use superlatives as the usual way of speaking, while others avoid them as much as possible.

For example, I suspect that the use of superlatives is another difference between American and English Canadian cultures. You may have noticed that, in comparison to other English-speaking cultures, Americans tend to use vocabulary that hovers at the extremes, from the *COMPLETE DISAS-TER*, on one end, to the *AMAZINGLY WONDERFUL*, on the other. The French and the Québécois also tend to do this.

– complete disaster　　　　　　　　　**amazingly wonderful +**

English Canadians (and, in my experience, French Canadians from outside Québec) tend to linger closer to the middle, in a range that goes from the *PRETTY BAD* to the *PRETTY GOOD*.

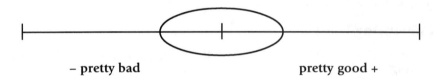

– pretty bad　　　　　　　　　**pretty good +**

I've heard Americans talk about how difficult it is to get English Canadians excited about something. My advice to Canadians, when listening to Americans describe something, is to apply the Monty Python rule of thumb and divide whatever they say by ten.[2]

By comparison, the English (particularly the upper classes) seem to have an even smaller linguistic range; they go from *NOT GOOD* on the negative side, to *NOT BAD* on the positive side.

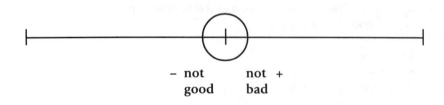

– not　　**not +**
good　　**bad**

---

2. This "dividing by 10" is from a skit in the British hit comedy television series: **Monty Python's Flying Circus.**

To influence someone using the Stress Response Influencing Language, you will need to choose the kind of language appropriate to the culture.

Summary
≋

Stress Response

Question: Tell me about (*a work situation*) that gave you trouble.

Feeling:	Emotional responses to "normal" levels of stress. Stays in feelings.
Choice:	Can move in and out of feelings voluntarily. Good at empathy.
Thinking:	Do not go into feeling at normal levels of stress. Poor at showing empathy. Keep cool in high-stress work.
Distribution:	Feeling 15%
	Choice 70%
	Other 15%
	(from Rodger Bailey, in the work Context)

Influencing Language

Feeling:	intense; exciting; mind boggling; wonderful
Choice:	empathy; appropriate, makes good sense and feels right
Thinking:	clear thinking; logical; rational; cold reality; hard facts; statistics

---

ℐ Wanna Do It *Myself*: Working Style

≋

What kind of environment allows the person to be most productive: working alone, with others around, or sharing responsibility?

The Working Style category will allow you to discover (or confirm) how you can be at your best; whether you want to share your work with other people, do it yourself while involving others, or work all on your own.

In this category many people have more than one pattern, a dominant and a secondary Style in a given Context. There are three patterns:

Independent

People who have an Independent pattern in the work Context want to *work alone* and have *sole responsibility*. Their productivity suffers if others are around or if they have to share responsibility. When interrupted, they may lose their train of thought. They prefer to work in an office with the door closed. At the extreme, they may forget to consult with others (especially if they are also Internal). At work, they can go for long periods of time without craving contact with others.

The expression, "A camel is a horse designed by a committee," was probably authored by someone with this pattern. As a manager, an Independent person will do most of the work by himself and probably not establish rapport easily.

Proximity

Proximity people want a *clear territory of responsibility* but need to have *others involved* or around, in proximity. They need well-defined responsibilities; to be productive and stay motivated, and their tasks must involve other people. Their productivity will fall if others share responsibility and authority, or if they have to work totally alone.

Of the three patterns, this one is most suited for people- and project-management positions. They will make sure that everyone knows what they are responsible for. Proximity people do well as the boss, or when they have a boss, as long as territories are well established.

Co-operative

Co-operative people want to work and *share responsibility with others.* They believe in the 2+2=5, the whole is greater than the sum of its parts, Synergy Principle. They have trouble with deadlines and finishing tasks if they have to work on their own. They do not need a territory to be in charge of, and as managers, will want to do everything *with* their employees.

The Californian light bulb joke describes these people. How many Californians does it take to change a light bulb? It takes six: one to change the light bulb, and five to *share the experience.*

Co-operative does not necessarily mean that the person co-operates, in the usual sense of the term, just that she needs to do an activity *with* someone else. When my oldest son Jason was about five years old, he spent an hour building a Lego boat. My youngest son Sammy, then about two and a half, came down from his nap and kicked the boat to pieces. Jason was very upset, but from Sammy's point of view, Jason had *the nerve to do it all by himself.* He did not wait for Sammy to do it *with him.* This was intolerable for Sammy, who usually did not go off by himself and play. He may sometimes be disruptive when he plays, but he needs the company.

Distribution _____ **%**

(in the work Context, from Rodger Bailey)		
Independent	**Proximity**	**Co-operative**
20%	60%	20%

Pattern Recognition
≋

Questions: TELL ME ABOUT A WORK EXPERIENCE THAT WAS (their Criteria)?

• wait for their answer

WHAT DID YOU LIKE ABOUT IT?

For Contexts other than work, you can simply insert the Context into the question: "Tell me about an experience in a relationship that was. . . . "

Make sure the person you are profiling picks a *specific example* of a situation that meets their Criteria. If they have numerous Criteria for the Context you are discussing, simply use one Criterion. Some people may never have had an experience that meets all of their Criteria.

For this category, you will need to listen carefully to what the person talks about. Listen to the answer for the first question and then ask the second question. Does the person talk about doing something *totally alone, in charge with others around,* or *together with others*?

Independent
- says I, I did it, myself, my responsibility
- won't talk about or mention other people
- the activity presupposes that they did it on their own

Proximity
- other people are present but "I did it"
- may or may not mention others, but the *nature* of the activity necessitates the presence of others (i.e. sales or teaching)

Co-operative
- will say: we, us, our job, together, etc.
- includes other people and shares responsibility

Here is how to ask the above questions:

SRC:	Sara, what was one of your Criteria for work?
S:	Challenge.
SRC:	So can you tell me about a work situation that had challenge?
S:	It was a performance issue. There was a question whether a *particular group of people* were performing at the level they were supposed to. *I had to define who was responsible and what to do about it* because the performance wasn't adequate. *I* had to pool that together in different departments and the challenge was to come up with the solution.
SRC:	What did you like about that situation?
S:	I used creativity, it was stimulating, there was a challenge.

In the example that Sara chose to mention, we know that others were involved so it cannot be Independent. Sara says "I" and clearly demonstrates an awareness of who is responsible for what. Her pattern is Proximity.

In the 1970s many of us learned how to say "we" and to "share our dilemmas." This is not necessarily an indicator of a Co-operative pattern. If it really is a Co-operative pattern, the person will talk about the fact that together "we" accomplished something, or that together "we" felt good. If the person indicates that this was his own responsibility, then it is the Proximity pattern.

Examples

Independent:	"I designed the new software and debugged it."
Independent and Proximity:	"I designed the new software and then with my team I got all the bugs out."
Proximity:	"I designed the new software with my team."
Proximity and Co-operative:	"I designed the new software with my team and then together we ironed out the bugs."
Co-operative:	"We designed the new software and debugged it. It was a great team effort."
Independent and Co-operative:	"I designed the new software and then we all sat down and debugged the thing together."

Alternate Question:

How long can you work alone in your office without phoning or going to see someone?

Influencing Language

You can figure this out all by yourself, and use it with other people, so that you will all work well together.

Independent
- do it alone; by yourself; you alone; without interruption; you'll have total responsibility and control; just close your door and reroute your phone

Proximity
- you will be in charge; others will be involved but this is your baby; you will direct; lead; your responsibility is X and theirs is Y

Co-operative
- us; we; together; all of us; team; group; share responsibility; do it together; you won't be alone in this (Away From); let's; we could do that

Team Players? Hiring and People Management

Many management and professional positions advertise for "team players," but what does this really mean? Most management positions require someone who can harness energy, orchestrate activities and create a vision for their team. These activities need a good dose of Proximity with only some Co-operative.

To understand what is needed in a position, you will need to look at the activities and the proportion of time spent in each one. Which ones are *do-it-aloners*? Which activities involve being responsible for the outcome with others involved, and which demand working together at the same time to accomplish the objectives? If the job requires a high degree of proficiency in all three, you are unlikely to find an ideal candidate and may need to redefine the position.

I had a job many years ago where I was the Assistant Human Resources Director in a national youth-development organization for a region that included the provinces of Manitoba, Saskatchewan, and Alberta as well as the North West Territories. My boss had a mainly Co-operative pattern and I have Proximity and Independent patterns at work. She had us decide everything together and I just wanted my *own files*. I needed to have a territory, something that I could be in charge of. She was highly satisfied by our working relationship and I was frustrated.

People who have a mainly Independent pattern at work need space and time to themselves. They excel in those situations that call for someone to keep plugging away by themselves, even when all hell is breaking loose around them. They can concentrate for long periods by blocking out peripheral activities. They do not fare well where constant communication and creating consensus are an integral part of the job.

Since about 60 percent of the population at work has a mainly Proximity pattern, you will notice that most jobs have been designed to give people their own territory as well as necessitating interaction with others. Where the division of tasks has been masterminded by a Co-operative person, there is little mention of individual responsibility, and this confuses and frustrates many employees. I suspect that the "open concept" design of offices was created by Co-operative types. More recently some companies have been experimenting with the "Virtual Office" concept. No one has an office to call her own. You simply reserve a space, depending on the nature of your activity. We'll see if this trend lasts.

Where an Independent person has had a hand in job design, they may have left out defining how people will interface and communicate with each other. This leads to "the left hand doesn't know what the right hand is doing" situation between individuals and departments, common in many organizations.

Pattern Combinations

I am often asked if there are relationships between two or more patterns in the LAB Profile. Is there a relationship between Independent and Internal? These patterns do not necessarily go together. You could want to work all by yourself, not know if your work is good enough, and have to ask, "Maureen, I've just finished this; can you tell me what you think about it?" (Independent and External), or I could publish a report and decide that it was well done, without bothering to get any feedback (Independent and Internal). Most of the patterns can go with any of the other patterns.

Summary

≋

Style

Question: Tell me about a (*work*) experience where you had (*Criteria*). What did you like about it?

Independent: Likes to work alone with sole responsibility.
Proximity: Prefers to have own territory with others around.
Co-operative: Productive when sharing responsibility with others.
Distribution: Independent 20%
Proximity 60%
Co-operative 20%
(from Rodger Bailey, in the work Context)

Influencing Language

Independent: you get to do it by yourself; you alone; total responsibility

Proximity: you'll be in charge; with others around, you'll direct; lead

Co-operative: us; we; all together; share responsibility; let's; do it together

---

Facts and Feelings: Working Organization

≈≈≈

> *How do people organize their work? Do they concentrate more on thoughts and feelings, or on ideas, systems, tools, and tasks?*

Working Organization is about how people work, either by getting the job done or focusing on feelings. There are two patterns in this category:

Person

Individuals with a Person pattern pay attention to the feelings and thoughts of either themselves or others. Feelings take on such an importance that *they become the task itself*. They will organize their work so that they can focus on people and their feelings. They are good at establishing rapport.

Thing

Thing people concentrate on products, ideas, tools, tasks, and systems (things). They treat people and ideas as objects, and believe that emotions have no place in the world of work. They want to *get things done*, and have a *task orientation*.

Distribution _____ **%**

(in the work Context, from Rodger Bailey)

Person	Equally Person and Thing	Thing
15%	30%	55%

123

Pattern Recognition
≋

Since 55 percent of the population have a mainly Thing preference at work, you will hear this pattern more commonly, although specific professions will have their own cultural pattern (i.e., many people in the human services professions have a Person pattern).

The questions are *the same as for the Style category*. In other words, when you ask the questions below, you will receive both the Style and Organization categories of information simultaneously.

Question: TELL ME ABOUT A WORK EXPERIENCE THAT WAS (their Criteria)?

- listen to the answer

WHAT DID YOU LIKE ABOUT IT?

Person
- speak about people, emotions, feelings
- will name people, use personal pronouns
- people are the object of their sentences

Thing
- talk about processes, systems, tools, ideas, tasks, goals, results
- will not mention people often except as impersonal pronouns i.e. "they", or "you"
- people become objects, parts of a process

Examples

Person:	"Mr. Richler was ecstatic with my report. I was quite happy with it too."
Mainly Person:	"Mr. Richler was ecstatic with my report. I was happy too because it meant quite a breakthrough for the whole company."
Equally Person and Thing:	"Mr. Richler was ecstatic with my report. It was quite a breakthrough for the company."
Mainly Thing:	"My report meant quite a breakthrough for the company. My boss liked it too."
Thing:	"My report meant quite a breakthrough for the company."

Other Questions: I recently discovered a test question that will allow you to verify when you are not sure.

"Imagine that you are working very hard to finish a piece of *very important work* that *has* to be done in *thirty minutes*. A colleague whom you *really like and respect* walks in at that moment, appearing quite upset and wants to talk *right now* about a personal crisis. What do you do?"

Either the person will choose to complete the task (Thing), drop everything to comfort the person (Person) or waver between the two, (Equally Person and Thing).

Alternately you could ask the person: "Tell me about a perfect day at work." The person will either tell you about tasks and things, or people and feelings.

Here is another example of someone who is Equally Person and Thing:

SRC:	Simon, what is it you liked about helping that person solve a problem?
S:	The problem is fixed. And the person is important.

Simon is paying attention both with getting a solution and with the person.

When you ask someone to tell you about a work situation that met their Criteria, and then ask them what they liked about it, they will usually reveal the element that has the most importance for them. The exception is when your interviewee knows the LAB Profile and therefore also knows what you are listening for. "Naive" subjects just give you their pattern.

Influencing Language

Just experiencing how great it is to use just the right words will help you achieve your goals.

Person
- use personal pronouns; people's names; feelings; thoughts; experiencing; this will feel good; for you; for others; the people; our team; our group

Thing
- use impersonal pronouns; things; systems; objects; tasks; objectives; process; get the job done; focus on the task at hand; the goal; the results

Good and Bad People?

Having a Person pattern is not an indication that you are either a "good" or a "bad" person. For example, if someone's profession consists of defrauding others, she would likely be totally focused on the emotions of other people. She will wind and weave emotions while spinning her web. Notice what Robert Redford and Paul Newman were doing in the film *The Sting*. This pattern simply describes *where* you put your attention.

In fine dining establishments, the maître d'hôtel treats all of the patrons basically like objects, placing them in their seats while calling for service. But his job is to make sure that these *objects* are happy. The best example of that kind of Thing pattern, for me, is on commercial airplanes. The flight attendants move down the aisle with the cart between them and you can see they are having a real conversation with each other. They're saying: "And you know what else I heard about him?" Then they plaster on a fake smile and bend down to one of the relatively immobile objects in a seat. "Would you care for a coffee?" You get your coffee and then they can return to their tête-à-tête.

Politicians also refer to people as objects. They talk about *the electorate*. What is the electorate? It is you and I, folks. But to them it is an object, a thing. When the Canadian people rejected the constitutional accords in 1992, many well-known national politicians explained the result by stating that "the electorate was cranky."

Hiring

At work, many jobs are organized to accomplish specific tasks and will need a mainly Thing employee. However, professional recruiters are increasingly looking for people who also care enough about feelings to communicate, establish rapport, and solve conflicts.

Some jobs do require a mainly Person orientation. Customer service and reception are good examples. They also need to have an External pattern, as their customers' feelings must come first. One of the secretaries with whom I worked had a strong Person pattern and was very fond of me. When I would ask her to do something, she frequently would drop everything and attend to me right away. I often had to tell her that it was not urgent and could be done the following week. She would also *not* do someone else's work right away, when she did not like them. In this case, she was also attending to their feelings.

Person salespeople often will have a hard time asking for a close. They are having a lovely time communing with their prospective customers and do not want to end it by focusing on the task at hand. Person managers run meetings that get off topic for long stretches to discuss personal war stories. "That reminds me of the time. . . . " Thing managers will sometimes not recognize feelings and may hurt or embarrass others, and then say, "Feelings have no place at work."

Many people choose counselling or social work as a result of caring deeply about how people feel. Sometimes they forget that the task is to help people become independent and then move on to their next *case*. When they have a high Person pattern, they risk becoming overly preoccupied with the emotions of their clients and suffering from burnout, (especially if they also have Away From and the Feeling Stress Response, which many do). For their own long-term well-being, these professionals need to create boundaries between themselves and their clients, and to focus more on the task at hand (without neglecting their clients' feelings).

In the training field, a survey of corporate trainers was done in the late seventies. It was found at the time that trainers tended not to worry whether they had achieved their objectives as long as everyone felt good. Today, trainers tend to be more task-oriented. Some people will say to me in a training seminar, "This material is very new for me. I don't feel comfortable." Since I tend to be more focused on the task at hand, my inside response usually goes like this: "So, are you being paid to feel comfortable?" However, as a professional, I usually respond by saying, "You know, discomfort is an interesting feeling, because it is a sign that you're stretching. And if you're doing something new that you're not used to, chances are you'll feel uncomfortable. Are you OK with that?" In my mind (with my mainly Thing pattern), making people feel at ease is a **means** to accomplishing the goal of learning.

Blake and Mouton noticed these two patterns when they discussed "Task" and "Maintenance" activities.[3]

Intimate Relationships

This pattern is also important in intimate relationships. Deborah Tannen[4] has noted that, in this Context, men seem to be more concerned with *reporting information* when communicating, while women in relationships tend to communicate in order to establish and maintain *rapport*. She calls this **Report Talk** or **Rapport Talk**. These patterns are similar to Thing and Person. I would suggest that to communicate with a Thing partner (be they man or woman), you could establish rapport by giving or eliciting information. To get a Person partner focused on something, you would want to concentrate on their feelings first, much as I did with the "uncomfortable" example.

Miscommunications between Thing and Person people can happen even over simple things. I was attending a course on Neuro-linguistic Programming in Paris and had lunch with a friend. As I was recounting a funny disaster that had occurred, Suzanne stopped me to ask: "But how did you feel?" "Alright, I guess," I replied, and continued on with the next in the series of mishaps. She did not respond to the funny events, but rather, "But how did they *feel*?" she wanted to know. "I don't know how they felt," I said, starting to become annoyed, "but this is what they did." The two mono-

---

3. Blake, R.R. and Mouton, J.S., **The Managerial Grid** (Houston: Gulf Publishing Co., 1964).
4. Tannen, Deborah, Ph.D., **You Just Don't Understand: Women and Men in Conversation** (New York: Ballantine Books, 1991).

logues continued. "That must have been difficult for you." "Yeah, I suppose, but what happened then was. . . . "

At informal social gatherings, you can usually recognize the Person people. They are the ones who continue talking to you as you are trying to leave. Sometimes they are loathe to break rapport and end your visit.

Sales and Marketing

Person people will buy something for how it will make them feel. Hair colouring and other personal products and services are sold this way. "You're worth it."

To sell to Thing buyers, focus their attention on the product or service and the benefits.

Summary
≋

Organization

Question: Tell me about a (*work*) situation that was (*Criteria*). What did you like about it?

Person:	Concentrate on feelings and thoughts. They become *the task.*
Thing:	Focus on task, systems, ideas, tools, things. Getting the job done is the most important thing.
Distribution:	Person 15%
	Equally Person and Thing 30%
	Thing 55%
	(from Rodger Bailey, in the work Context)

Influencing Language

Person:	use people's names; personal pronouns; feelings; thoughts; feel good; people like
Thing:	things; systems; the thing is; the goal is; process; task; impersonal pronouns

Why Middle Management Got the Squeeze When the Crunch Came: Working Rule Structure

> *What are the rules for behaviour that people apply to themselves and others?*

Rule Structure will give you some information regarding the ability or willingness to manage oneself and others. There are four patterns in this category:

My/My: My Rules For Me / My Rules For You

My/My people have rules for themselves and for others. They are willing to communicate their rules to others. Because they believe that people are similar, they think that what is good for themselves will also suit other people. They will say things such as: "If I were you, I would. . . . " A large majority of people at work have this pattern and probably in other Contexts as well.

My/.: My Rules For Me / I Don't Care

The My/. (period) people have rules for themselves and do not care about others. They do not necessarily harbour malicious intent toward others; it is simply not their problem or concern. These people often get on with what they need to do without thinking about others. Sometimes they are called selfish by others because they simply did not consider anyone else.

I was often awakened in the middle of the night in my sixth floor Paris apartment by people who I believe had this pattern. They would honk loudly at two o'clock in the morning, in a residential district, surrounded by hundreds of people who had, presumably, been sleeping.

No/My: No Rules or Don't Know Rules For Me / My Rules For You

No/My people do not know or do not have guidelines for themselves, but once given the rules, are quite willing to pass them on to others. As a result, they may have difficulty providing direction for themselves or making decisions. Instead, they may get stuck and not know what to do.

My/Your: My Rules For Me / Your Rules For You

People with a My/Your pattern know the rules and policies to follow at work but are reluctant or unable to communicate them to others. They operate from a "different strokes for different folks" perspective. Because they believe everyone is different, they consider it arrogant to tell others what to do. As a result, other people are often unclear as to their expectations.

These are the people who can understand both sides of an argument, as annoying as this may seem to those of us who take strong positions.

Distribution _____ %

(in the work Context, from Rodger Bailey)			
My/My	My/.	No/My	My/Your
75%	3%	7%	15%

Pattern Recognition
≋

You will need to ask these two questions and notice whether the person answers both or one only, as follows:

Questions:

WHAT IS A GOOD WAY FOR YOU TO INCREASE YOUR SUCCESS (at work)?

• listen for the answer

WHAT IS A GOOD WAY FOR SOMEONE ELSE TO INCREASE THEIR SUCCESS (at work)?

To identify these patterns, you will need to compare the answers to these questions. When someone does not know, they will hesitate a long time and respond with a questioning tone.

My/My:
- Same kind of answer to both questions or answers both questions easily.

My/.:
- Clear response to question one. Indicates lack of interest for question two.

No/My:
- Doesn't know the answer to question one. Has rules for question two.

My/Your:
- Has rules for question one. Doesn't know or wouldn't presume to say for question two.

Examples

My/My:	1. Work harder. Be more organized.
	2. Same way. Work harder. Be more organized.
My/.:	1. Be more organized.
	2. Not my problem.
No/My:	1. Uhm, ah . . . Not sure.
	2. Be organized.
My/Your:	1. Work harder. Be more organized.
	2. Everybody's different.

Influencing Language

If I were you, I would simply pay attention to what the person does because, after all, everyone is different, right?

While there are no specific words for this category, I have created some phrases to give you an idea how to match these thinking patterns in specific Contexts.

My/My:	"You would do that if you were him?"
My/.:	"You're sure about this and it doesn't matter for the others."
No/My:	"Now that you've been informed about what's expected, you can pass that along."
My/Your:	"You know what you should do and you want to leave it up to the others to decide for themselves."

Hiring and People Management

People with the My/My pattern are well suited for people management positions, provided they have the other requisite patterns: Proactive and Reactive, mainly Internal, mainly General, Other, Choice, and so on, (and the knowledge and skill, of course). They clearly state what they expect of their staff, and know and understand the rules by which they guide their own behaviour. If a job or a particular function demands that someone impart expertise, the My/My pattern is best. You would need to be able to tell others what to do.

In situations where a manager has an extreme My/My pattern, and particularly when combined with Internal, he can cause problems for the staff. In an organization for which I had done a large training program, the director decided that all the staff were to go through video-based training. His rationale was that this training had done him a world of good and would therefore accomplish the same thing for the staff. In my opinion, not everyone (at that level) was ready for that kind of experience.

When a manager has the My/Your pattern, she tends to create anxiety around her, because she does not *tell* others what she expects.

When it is important to discover the Criteria, values, goals, and so on, of someone and then work with those, a My/Your pattern is useful. My/Your people make good mediators and negotiators because they can understand each party's views while maintaining their mediator's neutrality. Much of today's standard training in listening and questioning skills for counsellors, coaches, facilitators, trainers, and therapists aims to create a My/Your pattern.

Sales people who have a My/My pattern do well, provided they also have the other desirable patterns for their work (Proactive, some External, mainly Procedures, Choice, Proximity, etc.), because they will ask for the sale. If they have an extremely My/My pattern, they may go overboard about telling others what to do. My/Your sales people may be reluctant to ask for the sale or make suggestions.

So, Why Did Middle Management Get the Squeeze?

The pattern often found in middle management in large, hierarchical organizations is No/My. These people do not typically set the rules for their staff; they find out what the rules are and pass them on.

Since the recessionary period of the early to mid-1990s, organizations have been going through many contortions: downsizing, "re-engineering" their processes, flattening the hierarchy, and in the process, pushing out middle-level managers, among others. Middle managers were perceived as adding little value to many processes, since they seemed to be merely policy and procedure *relay mechanisms*.

This function has been increasingly deemed unnecessary as electronic communication means become more sophisticated, times have been tougher financially, and competition pressures have increased from around the world. The role that middle management plays as people facilitators has been undervalued, in my opinion, as companies were looking to cut heads.

As a result of this process of elimination, a large group of people with a No/My pattern suddenly found themselves looking for work, some for the first time in their lives. What can we predict about these people? It is difficult for them. They haven't got rules for themselves about finding a new career or a new job.

Many support groups have sprung into existence specifically to help this group. They invite speakers to discuss job-finding strategies, raise one's self-confidence, and so on.

Telling Yourself What to Do

I had a career counselling client with the No/My pattern. I asked her, "Do you have trouble sometimes making decisions?" "Oh yes!" she said, "When they concern myself." I asked her to imagine that she was over there in another chair and then had her tell herself what to do. That solved a lot of problems for her. She had no problem telling other people what she expected but she had difficulty deciding what she expected from herself in the work Context.

My/. people do best where they can concentrate on the job to be done and not on others' needs. This kind of work is increasingly difficult to find, as many companies insist that their people communicate and co-ordinate their activities. These people sometimes take the "It's my way or the highway" approach and, if also Proactive and Internal, will bulldoze their way through whatever is going on around them.

I worked with the owner of a small environmental firm who had this combination. He had frightened most of his staff to the extent that they were convinced a pink slip was waiting for them at the end of each day.

Switching Contexts

It is possible to have a My/My pattern at work and My/Your one in a relationship. Since My/Your people do not usually state what they expect from their partner in a marriage, for example, it may be useful for them to switch into My/My from time to time just to let the other person know what they want or do not want. Similarly, people who spend most of their time in a My/My mode in their marriage may want to shift into My/Your to learn how their partner perceives the situation.

I believe that by knowing the different patterns, you can start to choose which one would be the most appropriate at a given time.

Raising Kids

In the Context of raising children, do you also find out from your children what they want, understanding them to be who they are, as well as telling them what you expect? In parenting, it is often appropriate to be in

My/My mode. It is also fitting at other times to use My/Your. One of the goals of parenting is to foster your children's growth and development.

Summary

≋

Rule Structure

Question:	**What is a good way for you to increase your success (at work)?**
	What is a good way for someone else to increase their success (at work)?
My/My:	My rules for me. My rules for you. Able to tell others what they expect.
My/.:	My rules for me. I don't care about others.
No/My:	Don't know rules for me. My rules for you. Typical middle management pattern.
My/Your:	My rules for me. Your rules for you. Hesitant to tell others what to do.
Distribution:	My/My 75%
	My/. 3%
	No/My 7%
	My/Your 15%
	(from Rodger Bailey, in the work Context)

Influencing Language
No specific phrases; just match the thinking processes in specific Contexts.

$\mathcal{D}$ecision Making Processes: Convincer Channel

> *What type of information does a person need to gather in order to start the process of being convinced?*

The information you will glean from the last two categories in the LAB Profile are especially important for sales people. The Convincer Channel category and the next one, the Convincer Mode, deal with how a person gets convinced about something. Until someone is convinced, they will not take the appropriate actions. At the moment they become truly convinced about something, they are most likely to buy the product or service, or to perform the task at hand.

For each given Context, people generally have a pattern about how they get convinced. There are two phases in this process. First, people will *gather information in a specific sensory channel*, (Convincer Channel), and then they will *treat that information in some way* (Convincer Mode).

Channel Patterns

See	They need to visually "see" a product, service or idea.
Hear	They need an oral presentation or to hear something.
Read	They need to read something.
Do	They have to do something.

Distribution _____ **%**

(in the work Context, from Rodger Bailey)

See	Hear	Read	Do
55%	30%	3%	12%

Pattern Recognition
≋

Question:

HOW DO YOU KNOW THAT SOMEONE ELSE IS GOOD AT THEIR WORK? (or How do you know that a car is worth buying?)

- **See**—have to see some evidence
- **Hear**—will listen or hear what someone will say
- **Read**—read reports, etc.
- **Do**—have to work with someone to know

Examples

See:	"Just by watching them."
Hear:	"When they explain their decisions you can judge their rationale and thinking process."
Read:	"I read their reports."
Do:	"I have to work with them to get a feel for how they work."

Sometimes people will have more than one answer to this question. For example, they may need to both *see* and *hear* evidence.

Applications

When you wish to convince someone about something, in a sales situation for example, or when assigning a task, you can simply match their Convincer Channel. If you know what kind (Channel) of information they need in that Context, simply give them the information in that form.

Examples

See:	"I would like to *show* you a sample."
Hear:	"*Sounds* alright, doesn't it? Is there anything else you need to *discuss*?"
Read:	"The *figures in the reports* are good."
Do:	"You'll want to *work with it* for a bit to decide."

Influencing Language

You can show a person what you are talking about between the lines, just the same way that they do it. Here is some sensory-based vocabulary for the above patterns:

- **See:** see, look, show, perspective, image, clear, clarify, light, dark, shiny, colourful, visualize, light up, vague, foggy, horizon, flash, get a look at, picture it, see it in action, view it, etc.

- **Hear:** hear, talk, listen, wonder, say, question, ask, dialogue, ring, noise, rhythm, in tune, harmonious, musical, tone, discord, symphony, shout, discuss, hear about, tell yourself, etc.
- **Do:** feel, touch, grasp, gather, in contact with, connect, concrete, pressure, sensitive, solid, closed, open, soft, link, hot, cold, warm, try it out, make sense, work with it, grapple with it, try it on, test it out, etc.

Summary

Convincer Channel

Question: How do you know that someone else is good at their work?

See: Needs to see evidence.
Hear: Needs an oral presentation or to hear something.
Read: Needs to read something.
Do: Needs to do something with the evidence.
Distribution: See 55%
Hear 30%
Read 3%
Do 12%
(from Rodger Bailey, in the work Context)

Influencing Language
Match the sensory channel (see, hear, read, do) with your language.

Clinching the Deal: Convincer Mode

> *What does a person do with the information previously gathered in order to trigger a conviction?*

After a person has gathered the information in a specific sensory Channel, they will need to treat it in some way in order to become *convinced* about it. This treatment is called the Convincer Mode.

There are four patterns:

Number of Examples

Number of Examples people need to have the data a certain number of times to be convinced, or to learn something.

Automatic

People with an Automatic pattern take a small amount of information and decide immediately based on what they imagine the rest to be. They jump to conclusions and, once decided, do not easily change their minds. They will often give the benefit of the doubt.

Consistent

Believe it or not, Consistent people are never completely convinced. Every day is a new day and they need to re-evaluate every time. I call this pattern the *Scarlett O'Hara* pattern, because "Tomorrow is another day."

Period of Time

Period of Time people need to gather information for a certain duration before their conviction is triggered.

Distribution _____ %

(*in the work Context, from Rodger Bailey*)

Number of Examples	Automatic	Consistent	Period of Time
52%	8%	15%	25%

Pattern Recognition
〰

Question: HOW MANY TIMES DO THEY HAVE TO DEMONSTRATE THIS (see, hear, read, do) BEFORE YOU ARE CONVINCED?

Number of examples
- will state a specific number of times

Automatic
- one example or assume people are good
- give the benefit of the doubt

Consistent
- never really convinced
- judge each time

Period of Time
- will talk about a duration or period of time they need

The question, as designed, asks for a specific number of times. People will either be able to answer that question or it will, at first, flummox them. Then you will know, by the process of elimination, that the pattern is *not* Number of Examples.

Examples

Number of Examples:	"Two or three times."
Automatic:	"I can tell right away."
Consistent:	"You have to judge each piece of work."
Period of time:	"Over a couple of months."

Here are some sample dialogues, to show you how to test to make sure.

SRC:	Gillian, how do you know that an equal of yours is good at their job?
G:	I just need to see and hear them once.
SRC:	Once?
G:	Yeah, I can tell right away.

There's a hint here. Sometimes you will get the answer to both the Channel and Mode questions when you ask the first one. Gillian needs to see and hear, and has an Automatic Convincer Mode.

SRC:	Jim, how do you know someone else is good at their job?
J:	I'll see what they've accomplished and hear good things about them.
SRC:	How many times do you have to see and hear that to be convinced that person has done a good job?
J:	Two or three times.
SRC:	(Let's test to be sure.) So if you saw and heard that twice, would you be totally convinced that they're good?
J:	Maybe.
SRC:	If you saw and heard that three times, would you be totally convinced?
J:	Yes (nodding his head).

Jim needs to see and hear; Number of Examples: 3

SRC:	Natasha, how do you know someone else is good at their job?
N:	I would want to work with them for a while.
SRC:	How many times do you have to work with them?
N:	Uh, I don't know. How long?

Natasha's Channel is Do; she also revealed her Period of Time pattern while answering to the first question, confirming it in her second answer. Now we need to find out how long she needs to get convinced:

SRC:	How long would you have to work with someone to be convinced that they are good at their job?
N:	Oh, a couple of weeks.
SRC:	So if you worked with someone for a couple of weeks, you would be convinced?
N:	Yes.
SRC:	Adam, how do you know that a colleague of your is good at their job?
A:	I read their monthly reports.
SRC:	How many times would you have to read someone's monthly reports to be convinced that she or he is good?
A:	Well every report is different. You could do a good

job on one and not on the next. You have to read each one.

Adam needs to read (Channel) and has a Consistent pattern for his Convincer Mode. He is never completely convinced once and for all; he judges each time.

Applications

Most of the population (52%) has a Number of Examples pattern (in the Context of Work), which means that they need to have the data a certain number of times to be convinced. Advertising often works on the theory that if you repeat a message six times within a given time period, most people will get the message and act upon it. Many personal development tape programs also recommend that you listen six times. The six repetitions will reach most people, because the majority need three or fewer to be convinced.

Consistent people take nothing for granted. Combined with Away From, this pattern is ideal in tasks that involve checking for mistakes or in any kind of quality control. You would not want Joe to think that, since he "knows" Charleen performs well, he does not really need to check.

Learning

Let's take education as a Context for a moment. A child is learning addition or subtraction at school and needs to repeat the sums twelve times to be convinced that she has learned it. The chances are that during school hours she will never get the number of examples she needs to convince herself that she can add or subtract. Lessons are usually designed with a certain number of repetitions of skill sets. If a teacher can detect how a student having difficulty gets convinced that she knows how to add, then exercises can be adapted to provide the necessary repetition.

This information can also be useful for parents to help their children with school work. "How would you know that someone can read well?" "When they can get all the words right away." (Channel: Do) "How many times would they have to get all the words right away for you to be *sure* that they can read well?" "Ummm, lots of times." "Lots? If someone could read all the words right away three times would you be sure?" "Hmm, I'm not sure." "Well, let's say they read all the words five times right away; would you be sure then?" "Yeah, of course." Then, as a parent, you can make sure that, at each stage of reading, the child counts the number of times up to five that they got the words. Once the child gets the *proof* they need, they will believe that they can do it and will read with more confidence.

You will sometimes need to discuss the proof with the child. If getting *all* the words or *always* getting the right answer is unrealistic, then maybe you could help them use a more attainable proof.

If a child has Consistent pattern (never completely convinced) in the Context of learning, you will notice that she will need to get convinced that she knows something *each* time she does that activity. You might want to point out that this time is like *each other time,* inasmuch as the child was able to do it, once again.

Tough Customers

Automatic people take a small amount of information and decide immediately based on what they extrapolate. In other words, they hallucinate the rest, then they decide. They are the sort of people who jump to conclusions or make snap decisions. If you are trying to convince an Automatic person of something and they say no in the first breath, do not bother going back to try to reconvince them. They only rarely change their minds.

As customers, Consistent people are the most difficult to deal with. You will need to re-establish your credibility each time you serve them. They may love your service one day and hate it the next and love it again the following day. They appear skeptical and just will not get convinced. Use the same Influencing Language as for an Internal person, paying attention to match their Convincer Channel. "I suggest you try it out before you decide" (Do, Consistent), or "Look it over and tell me what you think" (See, Consistent). This group is the most likely to return items that they have bought, or to change their minds on something they have agreed to in a negotiation.

Period of Time people need to have information over a set duration before they get convinced. Your customer may tell you that she needs to discuss (Hear) your product for a couple months. You can either wait for that period or phone her a few weeks later and say that you have been so busy, it feels like a couple of months have gone by.

Influencing Language

Each time you are with people, you can give them the benefit of the doubt that they will consistently take the time they need to make up their minds.

(Remember to also match the Convincer Channel)

Number of	
Examples:	(Use the number)
Automatic:	You can assume; benefit of the doubt; decide fast; right now
Consistent:	try it; each time you use it; every time; consistent performance; don't take my word
Period of Time:	(match the period of time)

Summary

≋

Convincer Mode

Question: How many times do they have to demonstrate (see, hear, read, do) this for you to be convinced (that they are good at their work)?

Number of
  Examples: They need to have the data a given number of times to be convinced.

Automatic: They take a small amount of information and get convinced immediately. They hardly ever change their minds.

Consistent: They are never completely convinced. Every day is a new day and they need to get reconvinced.

Period of
  Time: They need to gather the information for a certain duration before their conviction is triggered.

Distribution: Number of Examples 52%
    Automatic 8%
    Consistent 15%
    Period of Time 25%
    (from Rodger Bailey, in the work Context)

Influencing Language

Number of
  Examples: use their number

Automatic: assume; benefit of the doubt

Consistent: try it; each time you use it; daily; every time; use Internal Influencing Language

Period of
  Time: match the period of time

$\mathcal{T}$he LAB Profile Worksheet: Working Traits

On the following page is the second half of the worksheet to assist you in profiling someone's Working Traits. I have again included the indicators for each pattern to help you practise recognizing the patterns.

You can find a complete profiling sheet for both the Motivation Traits and the Working Traits in the Summaries section at the back of the book.

LAB Profile Worksheet: Working Traits

Name: _____ Company: _____

Profiler: _____ Position: _____

Date: _____ Context: _____

Questions	Categories Patterns—Indicators
(no questions for **Scope and Attention Direction**)	**SCOPE** ____ **Specific**—*details, sequences, exactly* ____ **General**—*Overview, big picture, random order*
	ATTENTION DIRECTION ____ **Self**—*short monotone responses* ____ **Other**—*animated, expressive, automatic responses*
• Tell me about a (*work situation*) that gave you trouble.	**STRESS RESPONSE** ____ **Feeling**—*goes in and stays in feelings* ____ **Choice**—*goes in and out of feelings* ____ **Thinking**—*doesn't go into feelings*
• Tell me about a (*work situation*) that was (*criteria*). (wait for answer) • What did you like about it?	**STYLE** ____ **Independent**—*alone, I, sole responsibility* ____ **Proximity**—*in control, others around* ____ **Co-operative**—*we, team, share responsibility*
	ORGANIZATION ____ **Person**—*people, feelings, reactions* ____ **Thing**—*tools, tasks, ideas*
• What is a good way for you to increase your success at (*your work*)? • What is a good way for someone else to increase their success at (*their work*)?	**RULE STRUCTURE** ____ **My/My**—*My rules for me/My rules for you* ____ **My/. (period)**—*My rules for me/ Who cares?* ____ **No/My**—*No rules for me/My rules for you* ____ **My/Your**—*My rules for me/Your rules for you*
• How do you know that someone else (*an equal of yours*) is good at their (*work*)? • How many times do you have to (*see, hear, read, do*) that to be convinced they are good?	**CONVINCER** ____ See ___ **# of Examples**—*give number* ____ Hear ___ **Automatic**—*benefit of the doubt* ____ Read ___ **Consistent**—*not completely convinced* ____ Do ___ **Period of Time**—*give time period*

Part 4

Applications

Applications

In this section, I have included examples of different applications of the LAB Profile. You will find lots of hints and subtleties on the uses of the questions, and on using the Influencing Language.

The following topics will be covered:

- Career Counselling and Personal Profiles
- Corporate Culture Diagnosis and Change Measurement
- Hiring Employees Who Perform
- Building a High Performance Team
- Negotiating
- Analyzing Your Target Market
- Political Campaigns
- Education and Learning
- Default Profiles

Career Counselling and Personal Profiles

≈≈≈

When people come to me for career counselling, we usually start by doing a LAB Profile. Also, managers have asked me to profile their employees to determine their strengths and weaknesses, either for the job they are presently doing, possible promotion, or transfer.

It is important to remember to establish clearly the Context with the person being profiled. Since most of the people interviewed do not know much about the LAB Profile, I usually include, in their report, the LAB Profile Summary, found near the end of this book.

Here are two examples of reports for career counselling:

LAB PROFILE REPORT
Bill X

Context: Work

Motivation Traits

The following patterns describe those things that will trigger Bill's motivation.

Mainly Reactive with some Proactive

Bill is more likely to think and consider than to jump into action. He is mostly motivated by situations where he gets to understand, analyze, and think. He may wait for others to initiate and feel more comfortable responding.

Criteria

The following words and phrases are his hot buttons about work. He will be motivated when he thinks of or hears them:

personal and professional satisfaction, sense of purpose, sense of passion, sense of excitement, sense of accomplishment, part of something larger, provides a purpose for my life, sense that I am empowering people and organization

Mainly Away From

His motivation is usually triggered to move away from bad situations. He is primarily energized when there is a problem to be solved, a situation to be avoided, gotten rid of, or not have happen. He is a natural trouble shooter. He will need to refocus on his goals at regular intervals to avoid being sidetracked.

Mainly External

In situations where he has to decide for himself, he can and will, but he doesn't have a particular need to be the one who decides. His motivation is triggered when he gets feedback, either from other people or from results. In the absence of such feedback he will become demotivated. He may accept information as instructions.

Mainly Options

Bill is usually motivated to develop new options, alternatives, possibilities. He often has difficulty *following* procedures, but is usually good at *developing* procedures. When asked to simply follow a procedure, he may try to fix the procedure. Breaking the rules is irresistible to Bill.

Sameness with Exception and Difference

He likes his work situation to change often. When he is sure that he knows his job, he is happy doing that job for a couple of years. For some aspects of his work life he likes to do a job for five to seven years; for other aspects he likes one to two years. His task clock seems to average at about three years.

Working Traits

The following patterns describe the work environment that Bill needs, the kind of tasks that suit him, his response to stress, and how he gets convinced about something.

Mainly General

Bill usually makes sense of his work as an overview and prefers to work on the big picture, but he can work with detailed sequences for extended periods if necessary.

Other

He accepts the emotional content of his communications with others. He has automatic reflex responses to the behaviour of people, which facilitates interpersonal communication. He makes sense of communication with others based on the nonverbal part of the communication.

Proximity with some Independent

Bill usually likes to work with others around and involved. To be most productive, he needs to have his own clear territory of responsibility. For some aspects of his work he wants to be totally alone, without interruption.

Thing with some Person

At work, Bill concentrates on the task at hand. While he recognizes the importance of feelings, given the choice, he will focus on the job to be done.

Stress Response—Choice with some Feeling

Bill initially reacts to job pressures emotionally, and may stay in emotional feelings longer than necessary. He is usually able to adapt to stressful situations and will respond based on his own belief of appropriateness. He is best suited to tasks where empathizing with others is an asset.

Rule Structure—My/My

Bill expects others to work the way he works. He has no difficulty telling others at work what he expects. He is well suited to people-management tasks because of this trait.

Convincer Channels—Seeing, Hearing, and Feeling

He is primarily convinced about projects or ideas by seeing the evidence or observing the product or process. He is also convinced by hearing or discussing it. To be fully convinced, he also needs to "get a sense" of something, a feeling.

Convincer Mode—Number of Examples

Bill is convinced by three to four examples. This is the number of times he needs to see, hear, and feel something to be convinced. Fewer than this number leaves him unconvinced.

Ideal Work Situation

The following points describe Bill's ideal work:

- time to reflect, analyze, and understand, with some time for initiating
- problem-solving and troubleshooting
- feedback in terms of results or by significant others
- possibility to create options, design new procedures; less apt to follow procedures himself
- evolution and revolution; wide variety of tasks and major change about every three years
- prefers to work on overviews, rather than detail

- with own territory of responsibility, others around; some time totally alone
- concentrate on ideas, tasks, systems, and some feelings
- avoid high-stress work

Suggestions

Bill needs to refocus on his goals at regular intervals. This will help him
to assess his present activities as to whether they bring him closer to his
goals and reflect his deeply held values.

Since Bill has an aptitude to create alternatives and to reflect at an overview level, he will need to team up with someone who is more Proactive
and more Procedures and detail-oriented to complete and finish the ideas
he will develop. To succeed at an endeavour, he will need to divide what he
has to do into steps, and follow them.

High-stress work with looming deadlines, for example, will not be
healthy for him over the long term.

≋

The checklist and suggestions at the end of the report can be used by
the client when evaluating choices.

Depending on the profile of the client, you can either suggest options
or give them a procedure for finding work, starting a new career, and so on.

Here is another sample report for a client who was considering moving
her part-time business to full-time:

LAB PROFILE REPORT
Claudia Y

Context: Work, present and future

Motivation Traits

The following patterns describe those things that will trigger and maintain Claudia's motivation.

Equally Proactive and Reactive

Claudia initiates or waits for others to initiate. She does either with equal
ease. She can be energized, while at the same time she can think and not act.
Understanding is just as important as action. She is just as likely to consider as
to act. She needs her work to provide the opportunity to do both.

To successfully set up and run her own business, Claudia will need to
actively engage her Proactive part, particularly to generate new business.

Criteria

The following have a high level of importance for Claudia in her work. They are her *hot buttons*:

always have things to learn, work with words and language, contact with the outside world, team work, well paid.

The experiences represented by these words are what Claudia is looking for in her work.

Toward

Claudia is motivated to move "toward" her goals. She is motivated by goals. She wants to attain, achieve, get, and is so goal-oriented that she may not recognize real or potential problems. She would benefit by having someone with a facility for recognizing problems help her when she is planning.

Mainly Internal with some External

Usually Claudia decides for herself and is motivated when she gets to decide. To a lesser extent she needs feedback from others to check how well she is doing, but generally Claudia knows within herself. She usually takes that information from others and evaluates it by her own standards. In her ideal work situation, she would have the opportunity to judge her work for herself, using feedback from others as input.

Mainly Options with some Procedures

Claudia is usually motivated to develop new options and find other ways of doing things. She is very creative. She may have difficulty completing procedures, because her main motivation is to develop alternatives. If Claudia runs her own business, it will be important for her to make sure that procedures are completed and that her ideas are taken to their logical conclusion before starting on a new project.

Sameness with Exception

She likes her work situation to progress and evolve. Claudia likes to do the same work for about five to seven years. She can accept changes once a year, provided they are not too drastic. This is an excellent pattern for building a business, as Claudia will stick with the setup and development phases, provided she is doing activities she enjoys.

Working Traits

The following patterns describe the work environment Claudia needs, the kind of tasks that suit her, her response to stress, and how she gets convinced about something.

Mainly General and some Specific

Claudia prefers to think about her work in an overview. She can work with specific details for extended periods. As a manager or co-ordinator of other people's work, she must remember to let other people focus on the how while she manages the general overview. She can see the big picture at work but deal with details when she has to.

Other

Claudia is sensitive to the nonverbal behaviour of others, such as voice tone, facial expression, body posture, and so on. She has automatic reflex responses to the behaviour of people. She makes sense of the communications with others based on the nonverbal part of the communication.

Stress Response—Feeling with some Choice

Claudia initially reacts to job pressures emotionally and tends to stay in emotional feelings longer than necessary. She is usually able to adapt to stressful situations and will respond based on her own belief of appropriateness. She is best suited to tasks where empathizing with others is an asset.

Proximity

Claudia likes to work with other people around. She likes to be the boss or to have a boss, as long as her territory of responsibility and authority is clear. Her productivity will suffer if she has to work totally alone or if she has to share the responsibility with others.

Mainly Person with some Thing

While at work, Claudia focuses mainly on people's needs. This means she will be responsive to clients' and her boss' feelings. She can also be task-focused. At times she may drop the task to take care of someone's personal feelings. At these times, she may need to remember the goals and decide on priorities, which she has the ability to do.

Rule Structure—My rules for me / My rules for you

She expects others to work the way that she works. She understands the rules and unwritten policies of the workplace and she has no difficulty telling others what those rules are, an essential quality for management.

Convincer Channel—See and Hear

Claudia needs to hear and see evidence when getting convinced about something. To a lesser extent she needs to do something with the product or person to input the necessary data to start the process of being convinced.

Convincer Mode—Period of Time

Claudia needs to hear, see, and do something consistently with the evidence for a period of six months before she is convinced. Less than this amount of time will leave her unconvinced.

Ideal Work Situation

In summary, Claudia needs the following elements in her work:

- opportunity to take the initiative and to reflect
- work toward goals (she needs to have elaborated specific goals or she will be demotivated)
- work that she can judge for herself with input from others
- opportunity to develop systems, procedures, and ideas
- progression and personal growth in five to seven year cycles
- concentrate on the big picture with a bit of detail work
- have the responsibility and authority with others involved
- rapport and empathy with others

Things for Claudia to Consider when Deciding on Developing Her Business:

- be proactive about prospecting for clients
- have someone help during the planning stage who can easily perceive potential and actual problems. Explain their role clearly to them
- make sure that the procedures needed to make the business a success will be taken care of
- evaluate the business ideas and make sure that each plan is completed
- plan for incorporating growth and development in the work she does

≋

THE KEYS TO PERSONAL PROFILES

1. Decide on the Context and the purpose of the profile.
2. Adapt the questions to the Context.
3. Describe the patterns using layperson's language for the patterns, when giving feedback to the person.
4. Make sure to include the ramifications of any relevant combinations; For example, with Away From combined with Person, you can predict that your client will drop whatever he or she is doing to take care of others' needs.
5. Test your diagnosis by asking the alternate questions when you are not sure.

Corporate Culture Diagnosis and Change Measurement

≋

There is a very simple, unscientific way to figure out the culture of an organization in LAB Profile terms: Ask the people who work there. In my experience, I have been surprised by the high degree of consensus among employees and managers about the profile of their company. While groups with whom I have conducted team building operations usually begin on agreeing about nothing, except that they have problems, they will instinctively know whether the organization has mainly Options or Procedures, Internal or External, Toward or Away From, Difference or Sameness with Exception, and so on.

At the IBM International Education Centre in La Hulpe, Belgium, the managers of management development from each country did a Present State—Desired State analysis of the LAB Profile of the corporation. They affirmed that the company had an Internal pattern, trying to shift to External, from Procedures to adding Options, and from Sameness with Exception to adding some Difference. This analysis enabled them to understand exactly what kind of attitudes their programs should be encouraging. We then worked on some of the strategies they were using and could use to those ends. (But that is another book.)

To accomplish the analysis, I simply described the attributes of each pattern and asked the participants where they thought IBM was. The process took about three hours and was achieved by consensus.

You can also use the LAB Profile to measure the effectiveness of organizational change operations.

Do a *before* corporate-culture diagnosis with a random group of people from the organization. Implement the desired changes with the appropriate strategies, paying attention to match your language to the Decision Factors patterns (Sameness, Difference, etc.) that are prevalent in the organization. About six months to a year after you have put the major changes in place, pick a different random group of employees. Have them describe the present culture using the LAB descriptions. The *effective* changes should show up by changes in the LAB patterns.

You can also design internal corporate communications after you have diagnosed the culture in LAB Profile terms. I will soon be publishing another book on this topic.

‌Hiring Employees Who Perform

An engineering and manufacturing company had advertised for a production manager. They received *300 applicants* and, out of that group, found *only one good candidate*. I was asked to profile the position and the senior management team to whom the successful candidate would report. I wrote their next ad with the appropriate Influencing Language, designed to attract the right people and turn off the ones who wouldn't fit. They received *100 applications* and *eight good candidates*.

Job Profiles

To profile a position, you will need certain information about the job itself, the environment, and the culture that the successful candidate will be working in.

For the position itself, you will need to understand what the specific *tasks* are and the *responsibilities* that the person will hold.

The following elements will help you determine the profile of a job. Does the job demand that the person:

- just go and do it / think about it / think and do (Proactive-Reactive)?
- manage priorities, attain goals / identify and solve problems (Toward-Away From)?
- decide by oneself, hold standards / adapt to feedback (Internal-External)?
- follow procedures / design them (Procedures-Options)?
- revolution, frequent change / evolution / maintain standards (Difference-Sameness with Exception-Sameness)?
- big picture / detail (General-Specific)?
- rapport with others (Other, Choice)?
- high / medium / low stress (Stress Response: Feelings-Choice-Thinking)?
- work alone / in charge of own territory with others around / together as a group (Independent-Proximity-Co-operative)?
- focus on feelings / tasks to be accomplished (Person-Thing)?
- communicate rules and own expectations / transmit received rules /

just get it done / understand both sides (My/My - No/My - My.- My/ Your)?
- check for errors, quality control (Consistent and Away From)?

Here is the job description for the Production Manager mentioned above. This company designs and builds equipment for the manufacture of different kinds of plastic film:

PRODUCTION MANAGER
JOB DESCRIPTION

Manufacturing Production Management:
Manage plant workforce through supervisors.

Balance plant production levels with sales requirements.

Determine manpower and material requirements.

Carry out studies on unit (trade category) loading, capacity analysis, and performance.

Monitor production reports and investigate causes of errors in production, shipping and data entry.

Release work orders to departments in accordance with master schedule.

Devise detailed production plans and schedule machine setups for trials and shipping.

Develop standard costing systems.

Ensure that shipments are properly done:
- completeness of order
- correctly crated/packaged/protected for shipment so that damage will not occur during shipment
- necessary assembly / electrical installation drawings are included
- shipping costs
- quality control

Interface with Engineering to establish priorities for jobs to be released.

Materials and Inventory Management:
Responsible for all WIP and stock.

Order and time deliveries from suppliers to co-ordinate with production requirements.

Maintain optimal inventory levels.

Co-ordinate and direct all activities relating to physical inventory audits.

Oversee bills of materials, determine production standards and part number.

Implement automated materials / inventory control system when feasible.

Co-ordinate / oversee purchasing department.

Negotiate prices / terms with major suppliers.

Select / establish new suppliers
Bring new ways / methods to make the purchasing function more effective and ensure that it changes to reflect the current environment.

Government Compliance:
Overall responsibility for compliance with applicable government regulations with the plant. This would include:

- OHSA—Safety compliance and due diligence
- Workers' Compensation
- hazardous waste removal
- WHMIS compliance
- evaluations
- discrimination

Facilities Maintenance:
Prepare annual budgets for supplies, spare parts, and accessories.
Establish procedure for equipment selection, operation, maintenance, and replacement.

Using the above job description, and having profiled the senior management team to whom the Production Manager would report, I came up with an ideal LAB Profile for this position. I have included it here to show how I write job profiles.

PRODUCTION MANAGER-JOB ANALYSIS

The following characteristics are to be preferred, based on the job description and the relationship with the directors.

Motivation Traits

Mainly Proactive with some Reactive
The job requires a high level of energy and the ability to initiate; to a lesser extent the person must be able to analyze and reflect.

Mainly Away From with a little bit of Toward
The successful Production Manager needs to be constantly troubleshooting, inspecting for errors, and making corrections. The directors will need to be goal-focused, with an eye on managing priorities.

Internal
The Production Manager will have to set standards and evaluate against these standards. To fully assume the workload, he/she will need to know

internally when things are good or bad, and not have to rely on the constant feedback of the directors. To work well with the directors, they must agree on a set of standards and how they will be evaluated, and then let the Production Manager get on with it.

Mainly Procedures with some Options

The Production Manager will need to be motivated by following procedures most of the time. He/she must be the sort of person who is compelled to complete and finish what he/she has started. To a lesser extent he/she will have to develop new procedures.

Sameness with Exceptions and Difference

The Production Manager will need to manage improvements and progression over time *and* be able to introduce new procedures and systems. He/she must also be able to handle a wide variety of tasks simultaneously.

Working Traits

Mainly General with a good dose of Specific

To work effectively the Production Manager needs to always have a handle on the overview. This would allow him/her to delegate when appropriate. However, several of his/her tasks necessitate that he/she handle specific details for extended periods. Normally a person who is equally General and Specific has a difficult time delegating, which could lead to frustration on the part of his/her staff, and burnout over the long term for the person him/herself.

For this reason, a person who is mainly General is preferable.

Other

The person must be responsive to tone of voice and body language to supervise and communicate with staff and negotiate with suppliers.

Stress Response—Choice

The Production Manager will need to be able to empathize with others and be able to control his/her internal state, to handle the work load without burning out when things go wrong.

Mainly Proximity with some Independent

Most of the tasks require someone who needs and understands the need for having a territory of responsibility while working with others around. For some of the tasks, he/she will need to work/think while completely alone.

Mainly Thing and Some Person

The person must remain focused on the task at hand and be responsive to feelings. Given ambitious production deadlines, the task must take priority over feelings.

Rule Structure—My/My

He/she has to be able to give clear directions.

Convincer—Consistent

Ideally, a person who is "never completely convinced" is the best choice for a position that demands quality control and inspection. This means that he/she will constantly check and not assume that things are okay because they were last week.

MOST IMPORTANT PATTERNS

Upon analysis of the job description, and taking into consideration the Profile of the three directors, the following patterns are the most important for the new Production Manager:

Mainly Away From
Internal
Mainly Procedures

I used the following comparison chart to compare each of the short-listed candidates from the first advertisement (that the company wrote), relative to the 'ideal' for the job.

COMPARISON CHART

PROFILE PATTERNS	PRODUCTION MANAGER	BOB	JOHN	MIKHAIL
Proactive-Reactive	Mainly Proactive	Equally Proactive & Reactive	Mainly Proactive	Mainly Proactive
Toward-Away From	Mainly Away From	Mainly Toward	Away From	Mainly Toward
Internal-External	Internal	Mainly External	Internal	Mainly Internal
Options-Procedures	Mainly Procedures	Mainly Procedures	Equally Options & Procedures	Mainly Options
Sameness & Difference	Sameness w/ Exceptions & some Difference	Sameness & Difference	Sameness w/ Exceptions	Difference & some Sameness w/ Exceptions
Specific-General	Mainly General & some Specific	Mainly General	Mainly General	Mainly General
Other	Other	Other	Other	Self & Other
Independent-Proximity-Co-operative	Mainly Proximity, some Independent	Co-op with some proximity	Proximity	Mainly Proximity with some Co-operative
Person-Thing	Mainly Thing & some Person	Equally person & Thing	Mainly Person & some Thing	Mainly Thing
Stress Response	Choice	Choice	Choice	Choice
Rule Structure	My/My	My/Your	My/Your with some My/My	My/My
Convincer	Ideally, Consistent	Consistent	Period of Time	Large Number of Examples, possibly Consistent

RECOMMENDATIONS

In my opinion, regarding the attributes of each candidate (not the skills or knowledge base), John is the most suitable, followed by Bob. I believe that John is the best because of his ability to perceive, predict, prevent, and solve problems and because of his proficiency at making decisions. He is the most likely to relieve the directors of many responsibilities.

Bob is more goal-oriented and may tend to overlook problems. Because he is more External, he is more likely to need feedback on a continuing basis to help him decide.

Attracting *Only* the Right People: Career Advertisements

To demonstrate how to write an advertisement, here are the two ads used for the Production Manager position.

The ad placed by the company before I was asked to profile the position:

PRODUCTION MANAGER

Private fast-growing engineering company manufacturing high-tech quality machinery for worldwide export has immediate opening for decision maker to manage production division.

Production to double within the next year necessitates efficient co-ordination of rapidly expanding department.

Right candidate must have minimum 10 years related experience. Emphasis on organization, planning, and purchasing. Candidates must have excellent people-management and leadership skills.

Here is the ad I wrote after doing the profiles:

PRODUCTION MANAGER

Immediate opening for a proactive Plant Manager who will grow with this engineering company, which manufactures high-tech quality machinery for worldwide export.

The right candidate will manage the production division, solving technical, people, and government-compliance issues by following procedures and developing new ones when necessary. You will set standards and assure they are consistently met, even under the pressure of ambitious delivery targets. You are highly experienced and skilled in project and people management and purchasing, and can prove it.

The first step is to call now for all the information you need.

I suggested that the candidates call, because only Proactive people will actually pick up the phone. Can you identify the specific Influencing Language used in the second ad?

ℬuilding a High-Performance Team

As a people manager, it is incumbent upon you to assess accurately the strengths of your people. Beyond being aware of their knowledge and skill levels, when you also know their LAB Profile, you are better placed to redesign or adapt individual task assignments (where you are able to do this).

One way is to list all the activities that must be done in your department, and verify that each one is indeed necessary and useful. (Many companies are now doing such task analyses with consultants to determine just what tasks are needed, given increased customer expectations.) Using the elements from the Job Profile section, you can list the ideal LAB Profile patterns beside each activity, along with the knowledge and skill requirements.

Once you have profiled and given feedback to each of your staff members, you can adjust task assignments based on what needs to be done and the profile of your staff. I suggest that you do this in a consultative manner, taking into account preferences where feasible.

Let's look at the team as a whole. What are the elements in LAB Profile terms that characterize your team? What are the strengths and weaknesses when you consider the tasks that need to be accomplished? How can you maximize these strengths? How can you attenuate, or take advantage, of the weaknesses when pursuing team goals and objectives?

This is an area where there is no one miracle recipe. Your team will first need to decide its vision, mission, and goals (within the larger context of the organization, of course). There are many books on the numerous available methods for doing this. The next step is to assess your resources (including your people) and evaluate where you are now in terms of performance. Any intervention you decide upon will then come as a result of comparing (1) your desired state and your resources with (2) your present state.

I would like to give you an example where I used the LAB Profile to help a team improve its performance. I assisted the department of pharmaceutical services at a leading-edge university hospital. After they had clarified, in both general and specific terms, where they were going, I profiled the entire team and the tasks to be accomplished.

Here is a comparison chart of what I found when comparing three Contexts—the *overall* work of the pharmacists, work in the *dispensary*, and the *clinical* work they do on the wards—with the group profile.

— PHARMACIST LAB PROFILE —			
OVERALL JOB	**DISPENSARY WORK**	**CLINICAL WORK**	**PHARMACISTS n=17**
Proactive & Reactive	Mainly Reactive	Proactive & Reactive	Proactive & Reactive
Mainly Away From, some Toward	Away From	Away From	Mainly Away From
Mainly Internal	Internal	Internal & External	evenly distributed between Internal & External
Procedures to Options (2 to 1)	Mostly Procedures	Options & Procedures	Mainly Options
Sameness w/ except & some Difference	Sameness with Exception	Sameness w/ Exception	Mainly Sameness w/ Except, some with double pattern
Mainly Specific & some General	Mainly Specific	Mainly Specific	Mainly General
Other	Other	Other	Other
Proximity	Proximity	Proximity	Mainly Proximity
Thing with some Person	Thing	Person & Thing	evenly distributed Person, Thing & both
Choice	Choice or Thinking	Choice	Mainly Choice
My/My	My/My	Mainly My/My & some My/Your	My/My

While it is obvious that there are strengths where the group profile matches the job to be done, and possible weaknesses where the patterns do not match, there are also other performance factors to consider. This particular group holds frequent departmental meetings to discuss how to work with patients, how to introduce and manage new technological developments and how to move the department towards its goals in improvement of quality.

Given that the group has a mainly Away From pattern, with about half highly Internal and mainly Options, I was able to predict what their meetings were like. A problem would be raised, and solutions suggested;then long-winded disagreements would ensue on what was wrong with the analysis and suggested solutions. Many members of the team were frustrated by the length, frequency, and lack of productiveness of these meetings.

We discussed ways to create more effective meetings by taking advantage of the strengths in the team. For example, they would need to discuss and agree on Criteria and standards to be met (Internal). "What do we want instead of the current situation?" They also specified what tangible evidence would demonstrate that standards had been met by asking: "How would we know we had achieved what we wanted?" Then they could explore options for how to get there. The Away From people would have free rein to examine the suggested solutions for problems and fix them. Lastly, the Procedures people on this team could ensure that the resulting tasks would be completed.

Interestingly enough for this group, given that the profile of their job had a good dose of following Procedures, most of the group fell on the Options side of that continuum. This may be an example that illustrates how one needs to take into account the culture of the organization. This hospital is a teaching and research hospital, known for its innovations in health care. Perhaps the institution itself attracts Options people to work there because of its reputation. I questioned the pharmacists about how they view their job. Do they see their day-to-day work as basically following procedures? Many of them said that each patient is different, with a problem that needs to be solved, as they search for *new options* with their multi-disciplinary team of doctors, nurses, and so on. I would like to be able to profile Pharmacists in other institutions to see if this group is actually different.

They recently hired a more Procedures manager to balance the team. She has contributed greatly by establishing more protocols and ensuring that they are followed. I continue to help them with hiring new staff.

While it is difficult to make generalizations about how to create a high-performance team, I believe that the starting points are a thorough knowledge of your team members and the jobs to be done. You will need to reflect upon the individual attributes of your team members in comparison to the mission, tasks and specific goals. (Am I My/My or what?)

Using the LAB Profile to do employee and group profiles, and comparing the profiles to the tasks that need to be done, will enable you to identify areas that need improvement and areas where your team can go from good to great. You will need to have some Options thinking about this, because no one step-by-step process will fit all cases.

Negotiating and Bargaining

While the LAB Profile itself is not a protocol for negotiating, it can be used effectively for understanding the needs and communication style of all parties. It will allow you to present your proposals in ways that your partners in negotiation can best accept.

At the risk of making a gross generalization, certain groups or sectors have identifiable cultures that can be understood in LAB Profile terms. For example, a combination found frequently in union bargaining units is the following: Reactive, Away From, Internal, Procedures, Sameness, and Consistent. People with this combination will react to management initiatives by noticing what is wrong (from their perspective) with any proposal, decide based on their own standards and Criteria, insist on following the same procedures to the letter, and protest loudly when conditions and demands change.

They tend to ask for identical treatment of workers (Sameness) and therefore will fight the introduction of systems such as merit pay (Difference). *Fairness* is a word one hears often in this Context. It is a Sameness word. *Fair* usually means the same treatment for everyone.

As a result, to negotiate effectively with a partner having the above combination, I would recommend that you give your rationale in terms of the problems for the workers that would be prevented or solved. As they probably have an Internal pattern, you could ask them to *consider* information on the disastrous alternatives. Forget about suggesting options. "The *right way*, to avoid treating anyone *unfairly*, would be to . . . "

Remember that if you are negotiating with people who have a Consistent pattern, you will need to re-establish rapport and credibility at each contact, whether in person, on the phone, or in writing. I put the Consistent pattern in perspective for a newly hired general manager. He was taking his company through a turnaround, starting in a situation with historically bad labour-management relations. "In order to convince your workforce that you want to make the company and the workers thrive," I told him, "you will have to prove your good faith many times. You will only need to screw up *once*, in their eyes, to destroy all the goodwill you have been creating" (Consistent).

For union negotiators, I would suggest that your proposals be put in Toward and Internal terms, listing the concrete benefits for them to consider. Management tends to understand and agree more readily to forward-moving, goal-oriented proposals. Management cultures also may have an Options pattern and not want to be tied down to following a given procedure, such as a collective agreement.

Preparation Is the Key

To get ready for a negotiation, spend some time analyzing your counterparts in LAB Profile terms. In cases where you have yet to meet, and cannot pre-establish contact by phone, look at any written communication you have received from them for phrases that resemble the Influencing Language patterns.

Alternatively, you could plan to ask some of the LAB questions in your first meeting, such as "Why is that important?" or "How will you know when this negotiation is successful?"

When I am negotiating, I usually assume that the person I am negotiating with has an Internal pattern in that Context, unless there is proof to the contrary. This assumption allows me to avoid being perceived as disrespectful, and creates a climate where both our views will be honoured.

Sometimes you will find that a person has an Internal preference in the Context of the negotiation but an External pattern to her or his perceived constituency. In this case you will need to use both sets of Influencing Language, while being careful to place each in the correct Context. "Only you can judge if your constituents will approve this," or "Having studied this to the depth you have, when you decide on the right answer, your people will show their appreciation for all the work you've done," or "What do *you* think about the impact this will have?"

The key to using the LAB Profile in negotiating situations is to take the necessary preparation time to figure out your counterparts' (and your clients', if you are representing them) main patterns. Your diagnosis will guide you in how to present or discuss issues with them.

⑭itting the Target: Analyzing Your Market

≋

Rodger Bailey, the developer of the LAB Profile, and I did some consulting for a major software company. They wanted to have a profile of their print advertisements (both media and flyers) to find out who they were reaching, and to test consistency within the advertisements. Specifically, we looked at two elements: the overall visual aspect (that which would first attract a person to look at the ad), and what was contained in the content (mainly text) of the ad.

We examined the ads and found that nine of the fourteen categories were represented. Here is a summary of our findings.

- **Level** (Proactive—Reactive): The ads matched the normal pattern for the general population at work.
- **Direction** (Toward— Away From): The ads were skewed in the Toward direction.
- **Source** (Internal—External): The ads focused mainly on attracting an Internal audience, although this pattern was not as clear as some of the others.
- **Reason** (Options—Procedures): The ads represented both Options and Procedures.
- **Decision Factors** (Sameness, Sameness with Exception, Both, Difference): While the ads generally showed a normal distribution (mainly Sameness with Exception),[1] the visual aspects of the ads were much more Difference than the body text. This means that people with a high Difference pattern would be attracted to the ad and then *not* find what they were looking for in the content.
- **Scope** (General—Specific): While a normal distribution is skewed towards General, the ads contained much more Specific data. Our client and ourselves felt that this overrepresentation of Specific matched the corporate buyer of software fairly closely.

---

1. Based on Rodger Bailey's findings

- **Style** (Independent—Proximity—Co-operative): The ads reflected heavy clusters around Proximity and Independent. We suggested that it would be useful to determine if our client's marketplace is actually shaped that way.
- **Organization** (Person—Thing): The ads contained a strong Thing orientation, which was probably appropriate for the Context.
- **Convincer Channel** (See, Hear, Read, Do): For the flyers, the visual aspects used mainly Do, while the text was mainly See and Read. Once again, what attracted the reader was not to be found in the content.

As a result of this analysis and an analysis of the desired audience, our client was able to determine whether their ads and flyers were reaching their target for the two products we profiled. By using data collected from their 800 information telephone line, they could test whether people with certain patterns were or were not responding to the ads.

We also demonstrated a startling fact for our client. I put the ads into two piles stating that one group had been written by one person and that the other group was written by someone else. This was verified by the account executive of their advertising company. We had clearly demonstrated that the writing was more influenced by the writer's profile than by the ability to reach a certain audience.

We would have liked to do more work with them to help specify the ideal Influencing Language for each of the products, based on re-interpreting market research already done into LAB profile terms. Unfortunately for us, our client, needing high Options and Difference at work, had left the marketing-director position and had moved on within the company. He now works for a competitor, in a different city. Plus ça change. . . .

Market Research

Surveying your marketplace can be done simply and inexpensively using the LAB Profile. You can do it by phoning your sample group. You will need to adapt your questions for the appropriate Context: toothpaste, using rail service, buying a car, and so on. You may well find, after profiling, that only a few of the categories are relevant for your product or service. You can then design your advertising or sales processes around the Influencing Language for the people most likely to buy.

Alternatively, if your product meets the needs of groups you are not presently reaching, you can switch some of your language and images.

You can also use the LAB Profile to re-interpret research that you have already completed. For one of the products in the software example, the *innovators* and *early adopters* segments of the market match the Difference pattern in the LAB. *Mid and late adopters* together, have generally the same distribution and behaviours as Sameness with Exception people.

The advantage of translating your research into LAB terms is to determine exactly what *Influencing Language* will be the most effective in your marketing campaign and sales literature.

Sales, Sales, and More Sales

You can produce extraordinary sales results by using the LAB Profile.

You will first need to adapt the LAB questions for your particular product or service. I suggest that you go through the list of questions and add in your particular Context, as follows:

"What do you want in a house?" or "What is important to you when you purchase software?" (Criteria)

"Why is reliability (their Criterion) important for you right now?" (Toward—Away From)

"How would you know if you did a good job at buying a car?" (Internal—External)

"Why did you choose your last life-insurance broker?" (Options—Procedures)

"What is the relationship between the place you live in now and your last one?" (Sameness—Difference, etc.)

"How do you know that a stereo is worth buying?" (Convincer Channel)

"How many times would you have to (see, hear, do, read) that to be convinced it's for you?" (Convincer Mode)

As you adapt the questions you will notice that certain of the patterns are more relevant to your product or service than others. In my experience, I find that paying attention to the Motivation Traits and the Convincer Channel and Mode are sufficient in most sales situations. Also, your product or service may naturally attract people with particular patterns in that Context. For example, rust paint is usually sold to avoid or fix rust problems.

When you are in the process of finding out what your prospective customer needs, you can weave the adapted questions into your normal conversational procedure. You will then know how to present your product or service, by matching their Criteria and using the appropriate Influencing Language.

By following this simple process you can shorten your sales cycle dramatically and increase customer satisfaction at the same time.

Who Can Sell and Who Can't?

Those of you attracted to multilevel marketing (MLM) businesses and other sales careers *solely* because of "unlimited income possibilities" (Options) need to realize that your chances for success are, in fact, limited. Those of you who would do almost anything rather than pick up the phone and speak to someone you don't know (Reactive), need either to overcome this obstacle or consider going into retail sales. Most of the time customers do not come to you delivered on a silver platter. This is your career, and it is in your own best interest to find one with tasks that suit you.

Most sales activities consist of *following a procedure*. For you to succeed in sales over the long term, you will need to be able to follow a procedure over and over again. This means having a mainly Procedures pattern in the Context of your work. For outside sales and generating new business you will also need to be in a very Proactive mode, to go out and prospect for new business.

Sales is a wonderful career for those of us who like to go out and take people through the process of finding what they really need and want. When you systematically use the tools in *Words That Change Minds* to help you satisfy your customer's desires, you will find that the results astonish you.

$\mathcal{P}$olitical Campaigns

≈≈≈

Political campaigns provide the most dynamic example of the LAB Profile in action. The 1993 Canadian federal election is a case in point: The winning Liberal party used language that precisely matched the mood and aspirations of the voting public.

The polls indicated that voters were very cynical about politicians, their campaign promises, and likely behaviour once elected. In LAB Profile terms we can interpret this as an Away From and Internal combination. The theme of the governing Conservatives was "We are *different*," relying on the pre-election popularity of their *new* leader, Kim Campbell. Wrong pattern. With the prevailing mood of cynicism, no one believed them. (Remember George Bush's famous pronouncement: "Read my lips. No new taxes.")

The Liberals produced their Red Book, with their commitments for governing after the election. Instead of telling people what to do (which would only work for people who are External), they told the public "we understand you are *fed up* with campaign rhetoric" (Away From). They presented their program from the Red Book and asked voters to *decide for themselves* (Internal). They also proposed that since they had put it all in writing, the electorate could *judge their performance* (Internal) once in power by verifying whether they had kept their commitments.

But the Liberal party went further than matching voter cynicism. They redirected the electorate by creating hope, with their positive visions for the future of the country. Contrast this with Kim Campbell's flat declaration that there would be no upswing in employment until the year 2000. Which party would you rather vote for?

The Conservative party not only lost its large majority but returned only two Members of Parliament to the House of Commons. (This makes the Conservatives the only party in the history of Canada to have achieved gender parity.)

The Notwithstanding Clause

Notwithstanding the impact of the language used, I am sure that the general unpopularity of the Conservative party, and particularly that of former Prime Minister Mulroney were important factors in the outcome of the election.

In the 1995 Ontario provincial election, the Liberal Party used the same strategy as their federal colleagues, producing a red book of promises. But the mood (and hence the LAB Profile) of voters had shifted. The Conservative party won a majority with their "Common Sense Revolution" slogan. Sameness AND Difference: the good ol' days as a revolutionary concept.

If political parties want to improve their chances of successfully communicating their message to the voting public, they might consider adapting some of the LAB Profile questions for their pre-campaign polls. These questions can also be used to judge the mood of the media, important potential allies in any campaign. The power of the LAB Profile lies in its ability to *measure the mood* of the public and *indicate the language* to which people will be the *most receptive*.

$\mathcal{E}$ducation and Learning

It is not my intention to criticize public-school education in this section, but rather to provide some food for thought.

Why are educational programs designed the way they are? It is usually because the authors believe they have discovered the *best way* to learn a subject. Often they are right about large percentages of the groups they hope to reach, but what about the smaller percentage of students for whom this is not true?

My comments are about these *other* students, for whom a given model does not work, and who therefore are more likely to drop out of school. In the work I have done with educators on the topic of reducing the number of dropouts in secondary school, we discussed strategies for keeping kids interested *throughout the school cycle.*

My advice to individual teachers in primary or secondary school would be to first identify the pupils who are not turned on by class activities. Secondly, profile them to discover what will trigger and maintain their motivation. Once the individual's motivation patterns are known, you can then adapt activities to suit their needs, using the resources and methods available, and inventing some when necessary. Lastly, you will notice a marked improvement in the participation and performance of these previously hard-to-reach students.

For example, Options students may have difficulty following the prescribed procedure, and as a result may become frustrated or disruptive in the classroom. These students are more likely to stay motivated and focused if they are given more choice and the possibility to develop their own process. Procedures students may have difficulty knowing how to start an open task. They would appreciate having a procedure to follow to get started. In each case you would need to make sure to use the Influencing Language that matches the student's pattern. "Think of all the possible ways to do this!" (Options); "Here are the first steps to get started" (Procedures).

You can also design or use activities to encourage flexibility in the LAB categories—following and completing procedures as well as developing options.

For Internal students to stay motivated they will need to make their own decisions. You can get them to evaluate their own work. When making suggestions to this group, you might want to use phrases such as: "You might want to consider," or "Can I make a suggestion for you to think about?" External students will need lots of feedback to know how well they are doing. To encourage the development of both Internal and External patterns, you can provide a balance in activities—self-evaluation (Internal) and adapting to feedback received (External). You will be able to see and hear who responds best to which patterns merely by observing the students' reactions to the tasks.

Much of someone's ability to use what they have learned is dependent on the *level of confidence* they have about having mastered it. When someone's Convincer patterns have been satisfied, they are more likely to use the material or do the activity more confidently.

If a child needs six or 7seven repetitions of a skill to be convinced he knows it, it is unlikely that he will get enough repetition in the course of a school day. My suggestion to teachers, when they notice a child feels unsure of what they have learned, is to ask the Convincer Channel and Mode questions. "How do you know when someone else is good at addition?" "How many times do you have to see them do it right (or hear that they got the right answer, or do the work with them, etc.) for you to be *convinced* that they are good at addition?" Then you can assign homework based on the number of repetitions or period of time needed. If the student has a Consistent Convincer Mode, (never completely convinced), you will find that she *knows* she can do it one day and perhaps is unsure the next. Remind her of the previous times when she knew she could do it. She is still the *same* person.

Adult Learners

Learning is a Context in and of itself. The act of *learning* something is about taking in new material and acquiring it for oneself, while *using* what one has learned requires a different set of behaviours.

As you can probably deduce, this process is a sequence of Contexts: Learn something new in External; evaluate it in Internal; use it and determine the results in Internal and External.

For someone to learn something *new*, she will need to be in an External mode. If someone is attempting to take in something new while remaining in Internal mode, the new material will find itself banging up against previously held standards and Criteria within the person. As a result, the ability to actually acquire the new material is limited. In many adult education courses, the learners are asked to put aside for awhile what they already know about a topic, to facilitate taking in a new way of thinking about it. They are invited to reinstate their critical thinking caps once they have mastered the material. However, I personally hate being told to leave my knowledge and experience at the door when I take a course, especially since it took me so long to acquire it.

You might wish to consider a more elegant way to help your students shift into an External mode for the *learning* part of the activities. Simply establish your credibility, so that your students become External *to you*. This credibility is particularly important for adult learners, as any corporate trainer will tell you.

In educational Contexts the LAB Profile is useful in two ways. First, it can be used to diagnose and plan for students who are not doing well with the programs in vogue. Second, it can help teachers understand what patterns they are *unconsciously* encouraging or discouraging as a matter of course.

Default Profiles

≈≈≈

Defaults are the standardized settings on your computer. They are what your computer *assumes,* unless you give it instructions to the contrary. It occurred to me recently that you can also use the LAB Profile patterns to make assumptions about people and situations that you may not have been able to research in advance. What patterns can you assume to be operating *unless* you get proof to the contrary?

For example, when I begin a presentation to a group of people whom I do not yet know, I find it useful to assume that the members of the group will probably have the following patterns:

- **Internal** to me: They are each wondering: "Who the hell is this woman and what makes her think she has something of value to offer to me?"
- **Away From** with regard to what I am presenting: They will notice faux pas, any inappropriate remarks, or examples that are not relevant to them.
- **Consistent**: They will like me when I say or do something they agree with and dislike me should I step out of line, with regard to their expectations.

Although these kinds of assumptions may seem negative at first glance, in fact they help me prepare. If I assume that a group has an Internal pattern (at least at the beginning) then I do two things right at the start of my presentation: I take steps to establish my credibility and I use Internal Influencing Language. "I will be presenting some information for you to consider in your work. I invite you to compare it to your own experience and decide what you think."

For the Away From pattern I suggest: "You know your working environment better than I do. We will have the opportunity to adapt these ideas to your milieu. I'm sure you'll notice which parts are appropriate and which *aren't*." To deal with the Consistent pattern, I constantly monitor the individuals in the group to notice signs of disagreement, confusion, and concern. I will invite someone with a concerned face to tell me what they are thinking, so that I can respond to it.

Once you know the behaviours associated with each pattern, you can predict the Default Profile for many situations. You can identify which patterns are *safe* to assume unless you get evidence to the contrary. I use the word "safe" intentionally: If you had unconsciously assumed the opposite pattern would a disaster result?

For example, you might assume (outside of your awareness) that a group to whom you were to present had an External pattern to you, just because they hired you. When you began your presentation, you might forget to establish credibility, presupposing that they believed everything you say. Under these circumstances, it is quite likely that you will be attacked on a substantive issue by a member of the group.

I often tell the students in my presentation skills workshops: "Only God can demand blind faith. Everyone else has to prove their case." Proving your case means both establishing your credibility and providing information to support your points. This will address the Internal and Away From patterns in your audience.

In sales situations, you can develop Default Profiles for your prospects and customers. Let's say you are a computer consultant. It may be safe to assume that many customers have an External pattern to you. They come to you for expertise and might run away if you asked them what they thought the best solution was.

The marketing group for a large pharmaceutical company presents their new marketing strategies quarterly to the sales representatives. We did Default Profiles for both the sales reps and the end customers: physicians. The marketing group felt that the sales reps had the following Profile when they were in the field, working their territories:

Mainly Proactive; Toward (focused on the sale); External (to physicians); Procedures and Sameness with Exception.

They also thought that the sales reps had a different profile when dealing with Head Office and the Marketing Group:

Mainly Proactive; Away From (picking holes in marketing strategies); Internal (we know the field better than those guys at Head Office); Procedures and Sameness with Exception (don't keep totally changing what we are supposed to do).

As a result of this analysis, the marketing group listed Influencing Language to use and to avoid in their presentations. They also redesigned their strategies to take into account the two different Profiles of the sales reps (for two different Contexts) and the customers' (physicians') Profile.

If you are a therapist or counsellor, you can assume that your clients have an Away From motivation when they come to you for help. You might consider using Away From Influencing Language in your promotional materials and when working with them. "You've decided that you are fed up enough with this problem to want to get rid of it, once and for all."

Default Profiles are an example of a Generalization. They are useful if you make sure to pay attention and adapt to the exceptions.

ᴡhat Else?

Words That Change Minds is the fruit of my experience using and playing with the LAB Profile in many different Contexts. It can help you just do things, as well as help you to stop and think about them. You will achieve many of your goals, while at the same time preventing and solving communication problems.

As you use these tools, you will notice what a difference it makes for the others you live and work with. The possibilities are endless for communicating in just the right way. You can make a big difference, improve what is already good, and maintain relationships that are important to you.

Whether you use the material in this book in great detail or just focus on the big picture, you will understand what is said to you and notice behaviours in new ways. This material can raise many passions and provide for rational thought. When you are working alone, with others around, or together in group harmony, you can feel great about what you accomplish.

If I were you, I would take these tools for myself and use them to guide me and help me understand how others are different. You will see, hear, and feel the improvements that working with the LAB Profile will instantly provide, over and over again, consistently, for as long as you want.

While I have discussed quite a few applications and ideas, I am sure that there are *many other ways* to use this tool. So I put the question to you:

"Now that you know how to understand, predict, and influence people's behaviour by finding out what will trigger and maintain their motivation, what else would you like to do with it?"

I look forward to hearing from you.

Shelle Rose Charvet
success strategies
1264 Lemonville Road
Burlington, Ontario
Canada L7r 3X5
phone 1 (905) 639-6468
fax 1 (905) 639-4220
Email: info@successstrategies.com
Website: www.successstrategies.com

Appendices

Summaries and Useful Bits

In this section you will find:

- LAB Profile pattern summaries and distribution figures that you can include in reports you give people
- An Influencing Language summary to help you plan what to say or write
- Research Abstracts
- Resources
- LAB Profile Worksheets to use when profiling people

I hope you have as much fun as I have using
Words That Change Minds.

$\mathcal{L}$AB Profile Pattern Summary

Motivation Traits

How a person triggers their interest and, conversely, what will demotivate them. Each pattern is described below in its extreme form.

LEVEL: Does the person take the initiative or wait for others?

Proactive: Acts with little or no consideration. Motivated by doing.

Reactive: Motivated to wait, analyze, consider and react.

CRITERIA: These words are a person's labels for goodness, rightness, and appropriateness in a given context. They incite a positive physical and emotional reaction.

DIRECTION: Is a person's motivational energy centered on goals or problems to be dealt with or avoided?

Toward: These people are motivated to achieve or attain goals. They have trouble recognizing problems. They are good at managing priorities.

Away From: They focus on what may be and is going wrong. They are motivated to solve problems and have trouble keeping focused on goals.

SOURCE: Does the person stay motivated by judgments from external sources or by using their own internal standards?

Internal: They decide based on their own internal standards.

External: They need outside feedback to know how well they are doing.

REASON: Does the person continually look for alternatives or prefer to follow established procedures?

Options: They are compelled to develop and create

procedures and systems. They have difficulty following set procedures.
Procedures: They prefer to follow set ways. They get
stumped when they have no procedure to follow.

DECISION
FACTORS: How does a person react to change, and what
frequency of change do they need?

Sameness: They want their world to stay the same.
They will provoke change only every 15 to 25 years.
Sameness with Exception: They prefer situations to
evolve slowly over time. They want major change
every 5 to 7 years.
Difference: They want change to be constant and
drastic. Major change every 1 to 2 years.
Difference and Sameness with Exception: They like
evolution and revolution. Major change averages
every 3 years.

Working Traits

How people treat information; the type of tasks; the environment they
need to be most productive; how they go about making decisions.

SCOPE: How large a picture is the person able to work with?

Specific: Details and sequences. They cannot see the
overview.
General: Overview, big picture. Can handle details
for short periods.

ATTENTION
DIRECTION: Does the person pay attention to the nonverbal
behaviour of others or attend to their own internal
experience?

Self: Attends to own experience. Doesn't notice
others' behaviour or voice tone.
Other: Has automatic reflex responses to nonverbal
behaviour.

STRESS
RESPONSE: How does a person react to the normal stresses of the
work environment?

Feeling: Emotional responses to normal levels of
stress. Stays in feelings. Not suited for high-stress
work.

Choice: Can move in and out of feelings voluntarily. Good at empathy.

Thinking: Does not go into feelings at normal levels of stress. Poor at establishing rapport or showing empathy.

STYLE: What kind of human environment allows the person to work best?

Independent: Alone with sole responsibility.
Proximity: In control of own territory with others around.
Co-operative: Together with others in a team, sharing responsibility.

ORGANIZATION:

Does the person concentrate more on thoughts and feelings or on tasks, ideas, systems, or tools?

Person: Centered on feelings and thoughts. They become the *task*.
Thing: Centered on tasks, systems, ideas, tools. Getting the job done is the most important thing.

RULE
STRUCTURE: Does a person have rules for themselves and others?

My/My: My rules for me. My rules for you. Able to tell others what they expect.
My/.: My rules for me. I don't care about you.
No/My: Don't know rules for me. My rules for you. Typical middle management pattern.
My/Your: My rules for me. Your rules for you. Hesitant to tell others what to do.

CONVINCER
CHANNEL: What type of information does a person need to start the process of getting convinced about something?

See: See evidence.
Hear: Oral presentation or hear something.
Read: Read a report.
Do: Do something.

CONVINCER
MODE: What has to happen to the information or evidence previously gathered to make a person become "convinced" of something?

Number of Examples: They need to have the data a certain number of times to be convinced.

Automatic: They take a small amount of information and get convinced immediately based on what they extrapolate. They hardly ever change their minds.
Consistent: They are never completely convinced. Every day is a new day and they need to get reconvinced.
Period of time: They need to gather information for a certain duration before their conviction is triggered.

PATTERN DISTRIBUTION

From Rodger Bailey's research, in the Context of work, the Language and Behaviour Patterns have the following distribution:

LEVEL			
Proactive 15%–20%	Equally Proactive & Reactive 60%–65%	Reactive 15%–20%	
DIRECTION			
Toward 40%	Equally Toward & Away From 20%	Away From 40%	
SOURCE			
Internal 40%	Equally Internal & External 20%	External 40%	
REASON			
Options 40%	Equally Options & Procedures 20%	Procedures 40%	
DECISION FACTORS			
Sameness 5%	Sameness with Exception 65%	Difference 20%	Sameness with Exception & Difference 10%
SCOPE			
Specific 15%	Equally Specific & General 25%	General 60%	
ATTENTION			
Self 7%	Other 93%		
STRESS RESPONSE			
Feeling 15%	Choice 70%	Thinking 15%	
STYLE			
Independent 20%	Proximity 60%	Co-operative 20%	
ORGANIZATION			
Person 15%	Equally Person & Thing 30%	Thing 55%	
RULE STRUCTURE			
My/My 75%	My/. 3%	No/My 7%	My/Your 15%
CONVINCER CHANNEL			
See 55%	Hear 30%	Read 3%	Do 12%
CONVINCER MODE			
Number of Examples 52%	Automatic 8%	Consistent 15%	Period of Time 25%

$\mathcal{I}$nfluencing Language Summary

Motivation Traits

LEVEL

    Proactive: do it; go for it; jump in; now; get it done; don't wait

    Reactive: understand; think about; wait; analyze; consider; might; could; would; the important thing is to . . .

DIRECTION

    Toward: attain; obtain; have; get; include; achieve

    Away From: avoid; steer clear of; not have; get rid of; exclude; away from

SOURCE

    External: so-and-so thinks; the impact will be; the feedback you'll get; the approval you'll get; others will notice; give references; results

    Internal: only you can decide; you know it's up to you; what do you think; you might want to consider

REASON

    Options: break the rules just for them; opportunity; choice; expanding; options; alternatives; possibilities

    Procedures: speak in procedures: first; then; after which; the right way; tried and true; tell them about the procedures they will get to use

DECISION FACTORS

    Sameness: same as; in common; as you always do; like before; unchanged; as you know

    Sameness with
    Exception: more; better; less; same except; evolving; progress; gradual improvement

    Difference: new; totally different; completely changed; switch; shift; unique; revolutionary; brand new; one of a kind

| Sameness with Exception and Difference: | (both sameness with exception and difference vocabulary will work) |

Working Traits

SCOPE

| Specific: | exactly; precisely; specifically (and give lots of details in sequence) |
| General: | the big picture; essentially; the important thing is; in general; concepts |

ATTENTION DIRECTION

| Self: | (keep communication focused on the content) |
| Other: | (influenced by the depth of rapport) |

STRESS RESPONSE

Feeling:	happy; intense; exciting; mind boggling; wonderful
Choice:	empathy; appropriate; makes good sense and feels right
Thinking:	clear thinking; logical; rational; cold reality; hard facts; statistics

STYLE

Independent:	do it alone; by yourself; you alone; without interruption; total responsibility and control
Proximity:	you'll be in charge with others involved; you'll direct; lead; your responsibility is X; theirs is Y
Co-operative:	us; we; together, all of us; team; group; share responsibility; do it together; let's

ORGANIZATION

| Person: | (use personal pronouns and people's names); feelings; thoughts; feel good; people |
| Thing: | (impersonal pronouns) things; systems; process; task; job; goal; organization; company; accomplishments |

RULE STRUCTURE

no particular words or phrases—you can match these patterns as you talk

CONVINCER CHANNEL

See:	(must see data to get convinced)
Hear:	(must hear data to get convinced)
Read:	(must read data to get convinced)
Do:	(must do it, or work with someone to get convinced)

CONVINCER MODE

Number of

Examples:	(use their number)
Automatic:	assume; benefit of the doubt
Consistent:	try it; each time you use it; daily; every time; consistent
Period of Time:	(match period of time)

$\mathcal{R}$esearch Abstracts

LAB Profile Inter-Judge Reliability

Inter-judge reliability of the LAB Profile was verified in two separate studies using the Statistic Kappa[1] (Cohen, 1986). In the first one, conducted in 1993, the data analyzed were obtained from recorded interviews with thirty-four subjects. During the second study in 1995, eighty-four people were interviewed in the Context of career decision making.

For each of these studies, analysis showed a statistically significant reliability coefficient for eleven of the thirteen categories covered by the LAB Profile. In both 1993 and 1995 the Stress Response category did not obtain a significant result, possibly because the judges worked from audio recordings of the interviews, and therefore could not take into account the noverbal communication of the subjects. For the 1993 study, the Scope category was also not significantly reliable. In 1995, the Level category did not give a significant result.

For each of the above-mentioned categories, there are no specific questions in the LAB Profile to elicit the patterns. In such cases, inter-judge reliability depends on the level of training and experience of the judges.

In summary, in both of the studies, ten of the LAB Profile categories obtained a statistically significant reliability coefficient: Direction, Source, Reason, Decision Factors, Attention Direction, Style, Organization, Rule Structure, Convincer Channel, and Convincer Mode.

These two studies demonstrate that it is possible to obtain inter-judge reliability for the LAB Profile categories that use specific questions to elicit the patterns, and that one can train judges who will get the same results from data obtained from the LAB Profile answers.

Étienne Godin, Université de Moncton

Cohen, J. (1960). "A coefficient of agreement for nominal scales." *Educational and Psychological Measurement*, 20(1), 37-46.

Godin, É. (1997). *Inter-Judge Reliability of the LAB Profile*. manuscript, Université de Moncton, Moncton, N.B., Canada

---

1. The Statistic Kappa was introduced to measure nominal scale agreement between a fixed pair of raters (p. 378, *Psychological Bulletin*, 1971, Vol. 76, No. 5).

The LAB Profile and Career Indecision

An exploratory study was done with sixty-one students aged between 17 and 24. The purpose of the study was to determine whether the LAB Profile would show differences between students who were able to make career decisions that they were comfortable with (n=41), and students who were indecisive and uncomfortable with their indecisiveness (n=20) with regard to career decisions. The students completed the Professional Decision Profile (Jones, 1986) and went through LAB Profile interviews.

The ordinal data from the LAB Profile interviews underwent an inter-judge reliability test (Godin and Sirois, 1995). Reliability was statistically significant for nine of the eleven categories used in this study.

The frequency distributions of the two groups were different on the following eight LAB Profile categories: Level, Direction, Reason, Decision Factors, Scope, Stress Response, Rule Structure, and Convincer Mode. From an analysis using McCullagh's regression model for ordinal data, these results were significant with a 95 percent confidence interval. However, in the Level and Stress Response categories, there was insufficient inter-judge reliability to have complete confidence in these results. There were no significant differences in the following three categories: Source, Style, and Organization.

While the results do not indicate that any of the categories fit one or the other group exclusively, they do show tendencies for each group. For example, while there was a high percentage of subjects in both groups having the Away From pattern, the percentage was slightly higher for the group who were indecisive and uncomfortable with their indecisiveness. Similarly, there was a slightly greater tendency to have the Sameness pattern, as well as a slightly smaller tendency to have the Difference pattern in the indecisive and uncomfortable group than with the decisive and comfortable group. However, these patterns were found within both groups. Also, all the people who had a Toward pattern were in the group who were able to make career decisions that they were comfortable with.

These findings, among others, have prompted the researchers to suggest that further studies on the LAB Profile and career indecision also include other elements. Apart from profiling the subjects, researchers should probably also include in their data whether the subjects have found in their environment the resources that meet their needs, as identified from the LAB Profile. For example, if individuals need to follow a procedure, were they able to find a suitable one from their environment? If so, how much more likely is it that they will be in the decisive and comfortable group?

Another aspect that might also be researched would be whether one can help the indecisive and uncomfortable people become more decisive by a judicious use of the appropriate Influencing Language.

Micheline Sirois, Université de Moncton

Godin, É. and Sirois, M. (1995). *Inter-Judge Reliability in 83 LAB Profile Interviews.* Unedited document, Université de Moncton, Moncton, N.B., Canada.

Jones, L.K. (1986). *The Career Decision Profile.* North Carolina: Lawrence K. Jones (instrument).

McCullagh, P. (1980) *Regression Models for Ordinal Data.* J.R. Statist. Soc.B. 42(2), 109-142.

Sirois, M. (1997). *Comparative Study of the LAB Profile Patterns in Groups of Decided and Undecided Individuals With Regards to Career Decision-Making.* Unpublished Master's Thesis, Unversité de Moncton, Moncton, N.B., Canada.

I appreciate all the work that Micheline and Étienne contributed toward legitimizing the LAB Profile and also wish to thank Dr. Lorraine Bourque, who directed this NLP research and gave them much encouragement. Thanks also to Dr. Réal Allard, who co-directed Micheline's thesis and provided many insightful questions and comments.

We spent many hours discussing the theoretical aspects relating to career decision and the LAB Profile, as well as the implications of the findings and the nature of the tools used to measure decisiveness and indecisiveness. We developed hypotheses on possible combination patterns that might make a person less or more decisive in the Context studied. After much debate and statistical analyses, we all felt that, while one could measure decisiveness (using Jones' test), perhaps decisiveness is actually a function of having one's needs met, whatever those needs may be.

But this remains to be proven. Anyone interested?

esources

Consulting and Training in English and French:

Shelle Rose Charvet
Success Strategies/stratégies de réussite
1264 Lemonville R oad, Burlington, Ontario, Canada L7R 3X5
Phone: 1(9 05) 639-6468 / F ax: 1(9 05) 639-422 0
Email: info@successtrategies .com
Web Site: http://www .successtrategies .com

Audio Programs:

Rose Charv et, Shelle; **Understanding and Triggering Motivation. The LAB Profile**, audio cassette series , available in English or French from Success Strategies .

Rose Charv et, Shelle; **Health and Metaprograms**, audio cassette series , available in English from Success Strategies .

NEW Internet-based LAB Profiling Tool for groups and individuals:

http://www .jobEQ.com — y ou can try out a sample test for y ourself.

The NLP Personal Profile and Guidebook, Arthur , Jay and Greg Engel.
Available from:

LifeStar
2244 S. Oliv e Street, Denv er, Colorado, 80 224-25 18 USA
Phone: 1(3 03) 753-9355 / F ax: 1(3 03) 753-9675
Email: lifestar@rmii.com

A written profile with similar content to the LAB Profile which can be administered to individuals and groups .

LAB PROFILE Consultant/Trainer Certification Program:
For locations and dates , please contact:

Success Strategies/Stratégies de réussite
1264 Lemonville R oad, Burlington, Ontario, Canada L7R 3X5
Phone: 1(9 05) 639-6468 / F ax: 1(9 05) 639-422 0
Email: info@successtrategies .com
Web Site: http://www .successtrategies .com

LAB Profile Worksheet

Name: _____ Company: _____

Profiler: _____ Position: _____

Date: _____ Context: _____

Motivation Traits

(no question for Level)	**LEVEL** _____ _____	**Proactive**—*action, do it, short, crisp sentences* **Reactive**—*try, think about it, could, wait*
• What do you want in your (*work*)?	**CRITERIA**	
• Why is that (*criteria*) important? (ask up to 3 times)	**DIRECTION** _____ _____	**Toward**—*attain, gain, achieve, get, include* **Away From**—*avoid, exclude, recognize problems*
• How do you know you have done a good job (*at ...*) ?	**SOURCE** _____ _____	**Internal**—*knows within self* **External**—*told by others, facts and figures*
• Why did you choose (*your current work*)?	**REASON** _____ _____	**Options**—*criteria, choice, possibilities, variety* **Procedures**—*story, how, necessity, didn't choose*
• What is the relationship between (*your work this year and last year*)?	**DECISION FACTORS** _____ _____ _____ _____	**Sameness**—*same, no change* **Sameness with Exception**— *more, better, comparisons* **Difference**—*change, new, unique* **Sameness with Exception & Difference**—*new and comparisons*

Working Traits

(no questions for Scope and Attention Direction)	**SCOPE** _____ _____	**Specific**—*details, sequences, exactly* **General**—*Overview, big picture, random order*
	ATTENTION DIRECTION _____ _____	**Self**—*short monotone responses* **Other**—*animated, expressive, automatic responses*
• Tell me about a (*work situation*) that gave you trouble.	**STRESS RESPONSE** _____ _____ _____	**Feeling**—*goes in and stays in feelings* **Choice**—*goes in and out of feelings* **Thinking**—*doesn't go in feelings*
• Tell me about a (*work situation*) that was (*criteria*). (wait for answer) • What did you like about it?	**STYLE** _____ _____ _____	**Independent**—*alone, I, sole responsibility* **Proximity**—*in control, others around* **Co-operative**—*we, team, share responsibility*
	ORGANIZATION _____ _____	**Person**—*people, feelings, reactions* **Thing**—*tools, tasks, ideas*
• What is a good way for you to increase your success at (*your work*)? • What is a good way for someone else to increase their success at (*their work*)?	**RULE STRUCTURE** _____ _____ _____ _____	**My/My**—*My rules for me/My rules for you* **My/.** (period)—*My rules for me/Who cares?* **No/My**—*No rules for me/My rules for you* **My/Your**—*My rules for me/Your rules for you*
• How do you know that someone else (*an equal of yours*) is good at their (*work*)? • How many times do you have to (*see, hear, read, do*) that to be convinced they are good?	**CONVINCER** _____ See _____ Hear _____ Read _____ Do	_____ **# of Examples**—*give number* _____ **Automatic**—*benefit of the doubt* _____ **Consistent**—*not completely convinced* _____ **Period of Time**—*give time period*

LAB Profile Worksheet

Name: _____ Company: _____

Profiler: _____ Position: _____

Date: _____ Context: _____

Motivation Traits

(no question for Level)	**LEVEL** _____ Proactive _____ Reactive
• What do you want in your (*work*)?	**CRITERIA**
• Why is that (*criteria*) important? (ask up to 3 times)	**DIRECTION** _____ Toward _____ Away From
• How do you know you have done a good job (*at . . .*) ?	**SOURCE** _____ Internal _____ External
• Why did you choose (*your current work*)?	**REASON** _____ Options _____ Procedures
• What is the relationship between (*your work this year and last year*)?	**DECISION FACTORS** _____ Sameness _____ Sameness with Exception _____ Difference _____ Sameness with Exception & Difference

Working Traits

(no questions for Scope and Attention Direction)	**SCOPE** _____ Specific _____ General
	ATTENTION DIRECTION _____ Self _____ Other
• Tell me about a (*work situation*) that gave you trouble.	**STRESS RESPONSE** _____ Feeling _____ Choice _____ Thinking
• Tell me about a (*work situation*) that was (*criteria*). (wait for answer) • What did you like about it?	**STYLE** _____ Independent _____ Proximity _____ Co-operative
	ORGANIZATION _____ Person _____ Thing
• What is a good way for you to increase your success at (*your work*)? • What is a good way for someone else to increase their success at (*their work*)?	**RULE STRUCTURE** _____ My/My _____ My/. (period) _____ No/My _____ My/Your
• How do you know that someone else (*an equal of yours*) is good at their (*work*)? • How many times do you have to (*see, hear, read, do*) that to be convinced they are good?	**CONVINCER** _____ See _____ # of Examples _____ Hear _____ Automatic _____ Read _____ Consistent _____ Do _____ Period of Time

© The Language and Behaviour Institute and Success Strategies ☎ TEL 1(905) 639-6468   FAX 1(905) 639-4220

ℐndex

≋

Adams, Douglas 101
Adult learners 186
Air traffic controllers 111
Airline pilot 66
Allard, Réal 213
America 46
American(s) 46, 114
Amnesty International 39
Analyzing Your Market 177
Analyzing Your Target Market 151
Applications 149
Architecture 67
Attention 100
Attention Direction 92, 103, 147
Attracting Only the Right People 169
Automatic 92, 139, 147
Automobile Association 45
Avoid a problem 46
Away From 16, 33, 38, 89, 189
Bailey, Rodger xiii, 7, 11, 13, 66, 177
Bandler, Richard xiii, 7
Bargaining 175
Being procedural 73
Blake and Mouton 127
Bodily ailments 60
Bourque, Dr. Lorraine 213
Break the Rules 63
Brotherhood of Maintenance of Way Employees (BMWE) 40
Burger King 59, 72
Bush, George 183
Buying patterns 72

Cameron-Bandler, Leslie xiii, 11, 13
Campbell, Kim 183
Canada Trust 59
Canadian Auto Workers (CAW) 40
Canadian federal election (1993) 183
Canadian National Railway (CN) 40
Canadian Pacific Railway (CP) 40
Canadian rail strike/lockout 40
Canadians 46
Can't Make Up Your Mind 28
Career Advertisements 169
Career Counselling 112, 151, 153
Cause-effect 28, 29
CERN (European Centre for Nuclear Research) 105
Change Measurement 161
Change Pattern 80
Changes in Context 36
Channel Patterns 135
Charlottetown Constitutional Accords 53
Cheap design 54
Choice 92, 109, 147
Chomsky, Noam 8, 11
Clark, Joe 53
Co-operative 92, 118, 147
Coaching and Counselling 75
Coca Cola
    New Coke 84
    Coke Classic 84
Combinations 97, 121
Common-sense Revolution 184

Computer Nerds 73
Consistent 92, 139, 142, 147, 189
Context 14, 17, 159
Contexts 61, 79
Continuous Improvement 84
Convincer 147
Convincer Channel 135
Convincer Mode 139
Corporate Culture
    diagnosis 151, 161
Counselling clients 133
Crisis management. 34
Criteria 16, 26, 27, 30, 31, 32, 57,
    65, 70, 89, 132
Crunch 129
Culture 40, 46, 161
Culture Clashes 69
Customer service 36
Cynical 34
Deadlines 41
Decision Factors 16, 77, 89
Decision Making 135
Default Profiles 151, 189, 190
Deletion 8, 11, 13
Delozier, Judith xiii
Difference 16, 77, 89
Difficult Bosses 100
Difficulty choosing 28
Direction 16, 89
Disassociate 112
Distortion 8, 11, 13
Do 92, 135, 147
Doctor-patient relationship 60
Doctors 60
Downsizing 132
Education 151, 185
Educational Design 56
Electronic communication 132
Employment Equity 30
English 114
English Canadian cultures 114
Environment 93
External 16, 50, 54, 55, 57, 89
Fate and Destiny 22

Faux pas 189
Fear of Success 38
Feeling 92, 109, 147
Ford Taurus 72
France 60, 67, 73, 101
Free Trade 53
Freedom from/to 39
Gain a benefit 46
General 92, 96, 147
Generalization 8, 11, 13
Giving Feedback 87
God 23
Godin, Étienne 211
Golden Handshakes 23
Good and Bad People 125
Goods and Services Tax (GST) 53
Greenpeace 39
Grinder, John xiii, 7
GST 53
Hamburger 59
Hear 92, 135, 147
Hierarchy of Criteria 26, 30
High Options and High
    Difference 80
High-Performance Team 151, 171
Hinting 103
Hiring 41, 56, 66, 82, 100, 106,
    126, 131, 151, 163
Hiring and People Management
    120
Honda Civic 72
Hospital(s) 67
Hot buttons 25
IBM 59, 83, 161
IKEA 70
Illness 60
Incompetency attacks 112
Indecision 212
Independent 92, 117, 147
Influencing Language 12, 55, 79,
    113
Insurance 45
Inter-Judge Reliability 211
Intercultural 57

Internal 16, 49, 55, 57, 58, 89, 189
Intimate Relationships 127
Irresistible Language 58, 66
I've Been Moved 83
Jaded 34
Jaguars 61
Jewish culture 46
Job Profiles 163
Key words 26
LAB Profile Worksheet 145, 207, 209, 213, 215
LAB Profile Worksheet: Motivation Traits 89
LAB Profile Worksheet: Working Traits 147
Labatt Blue 84
Laboratory equipment 59
Labour Relations 39
Language and Behaviour Institute, The 89
Language and Behaviour Patterns 12
Language and Behaviour Profile (LAB Profile) 5, 7, 11, 13, 212
Language Range and Culture 114
Learning 73, 142, 151, 185
Learning New Skills 73
Learning to read 31
Level 16, 24, 89
Life, the Universe, and Everything 101
Light bulb joke 118
M*A*S*H 105
Making Criticism 54
Making Decisions 26
Management 131
Management cultures 176
Managing Stress and People 112
Mandela, Nelson 39
Market Research 178
Marketing 69
McDonald's 59, 72
Medical professions 40

Meta Programs 8, 11
Middle Management 129, 132
Miller, George 8
Modeling 7
Model of the World 8
Mother Teresa 39
Motivation Direction 33
Motivation Traits 12, 87
Mulroney, Brian 53
My way or the highway 133
My/. 92, 129, 147
My/My 92, 129, 147
My/Your 92, 130, 147
National Action Committee for the Status of Women 39
Negotiating 98, 151, 175
Negotiations 39, 53
Neuro-linguistic Programming 4, 7, 127
NIKE 23
NLP 5, 7, 11
No/My 92, 130, 147
Nonverbal Indicators 110
North American Free Trade Agreement (NAFTA) 53
Number of Examples 92, 139, 147
Nursing 67
OECD (The Organization for Economic Co-operation and Development) 46
O'Hara, Scarlett 139
Options 16, 63, 65, 89
Organization 58, 92, 123, 147
Organizational Change 83
Other 103
Parenting 133
Passion 112
Patients 60
Paulsen, Pat 105
People Management 41, 57, 72, 82
Period of Time 92, 139, 147
Person 58, 92, 123, 147
Personal Profiles 151, 153
Pharmacists 40

Pies in the Sky 101
Plant Manager 41
Political Campaigns 151, 183
Positive Thinking 36
  or Negative Thinking 39
Possibilities 67
Poverty 38
Presentation-skills 190
Presenting 189
President Clinton 53
Preventative Medicine 40
Proactive 16, 19, 24, 89
Problem-solving 98
Procedure(s) 16, 63, 65, 89, 95
Production Manager 164
Professions Have Cultures 40
Proximity 92, 117, 147
Public-school education 185
Purchasers and Users of Software
  85
Raising kids 133
Rapport Talk 127
Re-engineering 132
Reactive 16, 19, 24, 89
Read 92, 135, 147
Reading Club 31
Reality 13, 40
Reason 16, 63, 89
Red Book 183
Report Talk 127
Research abstracts 211
Resistance 84
Responding to Feedback 54
Revolutions and Evolutions 82
Rogers, Carl 25
Rule Structure 92, 129, 147
Sales 181
Sales and Marketing 23, 31, 45,
  59, 69, 128
Sales, Marketing, and Submitting
  Bids 100
Sameness 16, 77, 89
Sameness with Exception 16, 77,
  89

Sameness with Exception and
  Difference 16, 78, 89
Saturn 84
Scope 92, 147
See 92, 135, 147
Self 92, 103, 147
Self-esteem 55
Self-evaluation 56
Selling 58, 61
Sensory overload 75
Sequence 95
Shift in Customers 58
Sirois, Micheline 212
Software designer 69
Source 49
Specific 92, 95, 147
Squeeze 132
Star Trek: Voyager 111, 113
Statistical process control 84
Stress Response 92, 111, 147
Style 92, 117, 147
Success Strategies 89
Switching Contexts 133
Synergy 118
Tannen, Deborah 127
Targets 41
Team Players 120
Telemarketers 66
Territory 117
Test your diagnosis 79
Thatcher, Margaret 49, 53
The Hitchhikers Guide to the Galaxy
  101
Thing 58, 92, 123, 147
Thinking 92, 110, 147
Total Quality Management 73
Tough Customers 143
Toward 16, 33, 38, 89
Transformational Grammar 8
Typing pools 83
UNESCO (The United Nations
  Educational, Scientific and
  Cultural Organization) 46
Union bargaining units 175

Urinary incontinence 45
Values 28, 132
When Bad Communication
    Happens to Good People 98
Where Do You Know That? 52
Whoofed Cookies Beverage
    Company 97
Wilson, Michael 53

Working Scope 95
Working Stress Response 109
Working Traits 12, 91, 92, 93, 145,
    166
Working with Groups 74
Writers' Block 43
YMCA 30